PEER POWER

Book 2
Applying Peer Helper Skills

Second Edition

Companion Books

    For Trainee—Book 1, Introductory Program, Second Edition
    For Trainer—Peer Counseling: In-depth Look at Peer Helping,
        Third Edition

Resource Audio Tape Available: PROBLEM SOLVING

Judith A. Tindall, Ph.D.

Psychologist-Consultant
Rohen & Associates
Psychological Center
St. Charles Missouri

ACCELERATED DEVELOPMENT INC.
Publisher
Muncie,   Indiana

PEER POWER
Book 2, Applying Peer Helper Skills

Library of Congress Catalog Card Number: 88-83298

International Standard Book Number: 0-915202-86-7

© Copyright 1989 by Accelerated Development
  First Edition copyright 1985

   2 3 4 5 6 7 8 9 10

Technical Development: Tanya Dalton
                           Delores Kellogg
                           Marguerite Mader
                           Sheila Sheward

Book Cover and Module Cover Design: Donna Johnson

Printed in the United States of America

Order additional copies from

Accelerated Development Inc.
Publishers   Tel (317) 284-7511
3400 Kilgore Avenue, Muncie, Indiana 47304

DEDICATION

To all the trainers who have used *Peer Power: Book 1, Introductory Program*, and felt that more was needed in terms of application of skills and awareness. Their ideas and encouragement gave me the energy to expand and revise *Peer Power: Book 2, Applying Peer Helper Skills, 2nd edition.* This hopefully will help "Peer Helpers" to learn more about themselves and others and to apply the skills learned in *Book 1.*

CONTENTS

INTRODUCTION TO APPLYING PEER HELPER SKILLS

You already have completed some beginning listening skills that have started to impact your life. You already have been utilized as a listener.

We believe that those skills you have learned are just a beginning and that you must continue to grow personally to be of assistance to other individuals. You have indicated an interest in the advance training; which means you have effectively demonstrated basic listening skills and responding skills. Now is an excellent time for you to move forward and learn additional skills, develop personally, learn leadership skills, and gain information that will help others.

As a result of many years as professional counselors, trainers, and consultants, we have attempted to offer skills that, through the years, we have found important in developing peer helpers. We believe that with the *Peer Power: Book 1, Introductory Program,* which you have just completed along with basic skills and with additional skills that you will learn in *Applying Peer Helper Skills,* you will become a more effective person and helper.

As you proceed through this phase of your training, continue to look at and understand yourself better. In so doing you will grow in self-respect and in ability to help others. As you become more open and able to confront others, you will be able to assist them with problem solving.

To work more effectively with different individuals, in Module 14 you will learn about drug and alcohol abuse, as well as procedures to help in intervention and prevention. The module on drugs and alcohol is designed to give you basic information as well as help you examine your own behavior concerning substance use. It also suggests positive ways to get "turned on" to helping others. You will be involved in role-playing situations where you can use your earlier skills of confrontation and assertiveness to develop an intervention.

As we begin to work with others, experiencing a variety of problems and stress, an important aspect is to understand your own stressors and learn effective management techniques; then you will be able to assist others in leading a healthier life-style.

Module 15 on Wellness Through Stress Management is designed to assist you in assessing your current ways of living and assisting you in getting involved in a behavior change program such as exercise, stopping smoking, and so forth. Many people with whom you work will experience many life changes such as moving from one residence to another, changing jobs, obtaining a divorce, losing a family member, and other life stresses. As a result, you as a peer helper with advance training will be assisting others who have major stresses in coping more effectively. We have found that people who are constantly under a great deal of stress often end up with either physical or mental problems. Module 15 will alert you to different ways to cope with stress.

To become a more fully functioning individual, you need to move toward developing your full potential—Enhancing Self Esteem (Module 16). To move in this direction, you must understand your values so that you know your value structure on certain issues and by so doing be able to gain more self confidence. The better able we are to perform as fully functioning confident persons, the more we serve as models for others. When developing your strengths and moving forward, focus on successes and do positive thinking. This in turn will assist you in helping others.

Often as you become highly skilled as peer counselors, you are looked upon to serve in a leadership role. With all the skills you have learned in human relations, you have probably developed new friends. Businesses, clubs, and organizations want leaders that are "tuned in" to others to serve as leaders. Module 17, Leadership Training, will assist you in becoming an effective leader. You must understand your own leadership style, know the manner in which you presently lead, and have an outline of the leadership style you want to be able to use successfully. Time management and understanding others are important as you work with others.

One of the most rewarding experiences as a peer counselor is that of a tutor. Helping others learn a skill can be difficult and rewarding. You will have a chance to understand your own learning style and ways to motivate others through activities in Module 18, Peer Helping Through Tutoring. Specific study skills are also presented. You will have an opportunity to develop techniques for tutoring others.

As a leader you will be called on to lead discussion groups and you will be expected to enable the group to be productive in its decisions. At times you will be expected to listen to people that would like to talk. Facilitating Small Discussion Groups (Module 19) will be another major aspect of your development as a peer helper. Discussion skills can be used with small groups toward better understanding of certain issues. Discussion groups have been used in schools for one of the prevention approaches to substance abuse, value clarification activities, and additional topics. Discussion groups have been used in business in "quality circles" to help employees be more involved in the business. In organizations discussion groups are used to help people to make decisions concerning different issues. Additional leadership skills of setting action plans and public relations can be used in applying peer helping skills.

At times you will be asked to lead whole classroom groups on health issues, value clarification issues and other issues. You will practice using these skills in Module 20, Leading Classroom Groups. As you lead large groups your basic communication skills are important. You also need additional skills in public speaking, motivation, planning and organization.

Eating disorders is a problem that is on the rise. Part of the reason is the emphasis in our society toward thinness. Poor eating habits coupled with addictive behavior often leads to bulimia, aneorexia, and compulsive overeating, Module 21. You will have an opportunity to look at your own eating habits and recognize habits in others that are unhealthy.

Suicide is the second leading cause of death for adolescents—accidents being first. Most people have known someone that is considering suicide or has completed suicide. Peer helpers are often the first to come in contact with potential suicide victims and also deal with survivors. In Module 22, Suicide Prevention, you will learn intervention techniques.

Loss of one kind or another is experienced by all people. Loss as caused by death, move, injury, or illness has tremendous impact on people. Peer helpers are tremendous resources to others experiencing loss. In Module 23, Coping With Loss, you will learn more about offering support to others.

As peer counselors/peer helpers start training, peer helpers ethical issues will need to be discussed and certified. The National Peer Helpers Association has developed a Code of Ethics for the Peer Helpers. Local groups need to develop a Code of Ethics and a Code of Conduct. These are discussed in Module 24, Ethical Considerations in Peer Counseling.

As you put your skills into action and start an effective peer counseling program, you may find that you need to review some skills and may need additional information to perform your job. You will also find that just talking with other peer counselors is very supportive. You may want to form organizations and attend meetings that focus just on peer counseling skills and share your expertise.

As you perform your job, the need for more skills may occur. If organizing a formal class would be helpful, provide feedback to your trainer who may assist you in continuation of your development toward a more effective peer counselor.

Good luck with your new skills and keep growing and learning. We would like to hear about your successes and problems. Please write me, Dr. Judith A. Tindall, the author, at Accelerated Development Incorporated, 3400 Kilgore Avenue, Muncie, Indiana 47304. We will respond to you. . . . . It is nice to begin to develop a network of peer counselors. You are entering into an exciting new way of thinking and behaving and one that you may use all of your life. A whole new future awaits you. . . .

Judith A. Tindall

MODULE XIV

DRUGS AND ALCOHOL ABUSE— INTERVENTION and PREVENTION

DRUGS AND ALCOHOL ABUSE

INTERVENTION AND PREVENTION

Once you have received your basic communication skills training and have your peer counseling program in operation, an important next step is to turn to other issues that will help you become a more effective helper. The next few modules are designed to give you additional training in areas in which you are most interested.

This module deals with how peer helpers can aid in drug and alcohol intervention and prevention. As a peer helper, recognize and assume responsibility for four things you can do. First, one must be able to recognize that a drug or alcohol problem does exist. Second, be able to recognize a person who has such a problem. Third, be able to get the person to professional help. Fourth, be helpful in working with persons who have been through treatment and are back in their original environment. Those persons will need assistance in maintaining their sobriety and in finding new friends and new activities. This module could best be used by high school and older peer counselors.

America is a nation of drug abusers. While the common picture of drug abusers is long-haired, spaced-out hippies, or the falling-down drunks, in reality they are far from this stereotype. Look at your own lifestyle.

- How many cups of coffee do you need to get started?

- How many cigarettes do you smoke in a day?

- How many cokes or other soft drinks with caffeine do you drink in a day?

- Do you take a tranquilizer when you feel uptight?

America is a pill-conscious society. The problem with drugs—prescribed or otherwise—is that they often mask real problems. We can identify and treat those problems that cause a person to abuse drugs.

Of the 100 million Americans who use alcohol, one in twelve will develop the disease of alcoholism. It can affect anyone, regardless of race, occupation, marital status, or personal situation. It has nothing to do with willpower or morality; it may be merely a symptom of other, deeper problems. Although the disease can be arrested, as yet no known cure exists, but researchers are continuing to look into the causes of alcoholism.

Alcoholism is an addictive disease. The alcoholic has a physical and psychological dependence on the drug alcohol. The only way to help alcoholics is to get them to realize and admit to themselves that they can live happily and comfortably without the use of alcohol. Family members often must get help for themselves also, lest they be devastated by trying to deal with the alcoholic's disease. Families have special needs, Adult children of Alcoholics, Al-Anons and Alateens are all support groups designed to assist family members of the abuser.

Using is different than abusing drugs. For alcohol and drug problems to exist, the person must first have made a personal decision to ingest the chemical to an extreme degree. In general three levels of personal involvement exist, each having its own unique states, motivation, and consequences. The first level is use. The second, abuse, is the critical trouble level. Finally comes dependence, the chronic level, which results in loss of control. As involvement with the drug intensifies, the drug becomes increasingly vital to the user's lifestyle. Therefore, an important first step is to obtain information about drugs and alcohol and how they affect others' lives as well as yours.

Use. This module needs extra reading and outside help; professional drug and alcohol counselors, Al-Anon, and AA are possible outside resources. This module can be used with older high school students and adults. It also can be used with the confrontation module. Reference books for those who want to explore: Joseph Perez, *Counseling the Alcoholic,* 1985, Accelerated Development Inc., Muncie, IN. Joseph Perez, Coping Within The Alcoholic Family, 1986, Accelerated Development Inc., Muncie, IN.

Name _____

Date _____ Hour _____

CHECKING MY KNOWLEDGE OF DRUGS AND ALCOHOL

GOALS

In this exercise you will learn

1. some of the symptoms of alcoholism,

2. some common signs of other drug use, and

3. ways to test your understanding of drugs and alcohol.

DIRECTIONS

1. Look over the following *"Twenty-Six Questions."* Think of someone you know, and see if you can identify any of the symptoms of alcoholism in that person.

2. Look over the list of *"Common Signs of Other Drug Use."*

3. Take the short *"Drug and Alcohol Review Quiz"* to check your knowledge of use and abuse.

4. Work the "Word Puzzle."

TWENTY-SIX QUESTIONS:
POSSIBLE SYMPTOMS OF ALCOHOLISM
ARRANGED IN ORDER OF INCREASING DEPENDENCE

Yes   No

1. Do you occasionally drink heavily after a disappointment, a quarrel, or when the boss gives you a hard time?

2. Do you always drink more heavily than usual when you have trouble or feel under pressure?

3. Have you noticed that you are able to handle more liquor than you did when you were first drinking?

4. Did you ever wake up on the "morning after" and find that you could not remember part of the past evening, even though your friends say you did not pass out?

5. Do you try to have a few extra drinks the others will not know of when you are drinking with other people?

6. Are there certain occasions when you would feel uncomfortable if alcohol were not available?

7. Have you noticed recently that you are more anxious to get the first drink than you used to be?

8. Do you sometimes feel a little guilty about your drinking?

Yes	No	
___	_✓_	9. Are you secretly irritated when your family or friends discuss your drinking?
___	_✓_	10. Have you recently noticed an increase in frequency of your memory blackouts?
_✓_	___	11. Do you often find that you wish to continue drinking after friends say they have had enough?
___	_✓_	12. Do you usually have a reason for the occasions when you drink heavily?
___	_✓_	13. Do you often, when sober, regret the things you have done or said while drinking?
___	_✓_	14. Have you tried switching brands or following various plans to control your drinking?
___	_✓_	15. Have you often failed to keep the promises made to yourself about controlling or cutting down on your drinking?
___	_✓_	16. Have you ever tried to control your drinking by changing jobs or by moving?
_✓_	___	17. Do you try to avoid your family or close friends while you are drinking?
___	_✓_	18. Are you having an increasing number of financial and work problems?
___	_✓_	19. Do more people seem to be treating you unfairly without good reason?
___	_✓_	20. Do you eat very little or irregularly when you are drinking?
___	_✓_	21. Do you sometimes have the shakes in the morning and find that it helps to have a little drink?
___	_✓_	22. Have you recently noticed that you cannot drink as much as you once did?
___	_✓_	23. Do you sometimes lose days at a time?
_✓_	___	24. Do you sometimes feel very depressed and wonder whether life is worth living?
___	_✓_	25. Do you sometimes see or hear things that aren't there after periods of drinking?
___	_✓_	26. Do you get terribly frightened after you have been drinking heavily?

If the answer is "Yes" to any of these questions, possible symptoms of alcoholism are indicated. Yes answers to several questions indicate various stages of alcoholism. Several yes answers to questions No.1 through No.8 may indicate an early stage; to questions No.9 through No.21, the middle stage; and to questions No.22 through No.26, a later stage.

(Source: The National Council on Alcoholism.)

Exercise 14.1 (Continued)

Name _____

Date _____ Hour _____

COMMON SIGNS OF OTHER DRUG USE

The information that follows includes symptoms and danger signals of such things as glue sniffing and the use of heroin or marijuana. The listed symptoms or changes in behavior do not necessarily indicate that the individual has become a user but that the person should certainly be on the alert.

Drug: **Marijuana (Pot, Grass)**

Physical symptoms: Sleepiness, wandering mind, enlarged pupils, lack of coordination, craving for sweets, increased appetite.

Look for: Strong odor of burnt leaves, discolored fingers, physical evidence (papers, roach clip, pot pipe).

Drug: **Amphetamines, Pep Pills (Uppers)**

Physical symptoms: Aggressive behavior, silliness, rapid speech, confused thinking, no appetite, extreme fatigue, shakiness.

Look for: Chain smoking, presence of pills of various colors.

Drug: **Barbituates (Downers)**

Physical symptoms: Drowsiness, stupor, dullness, slurred speech, drunk appearance, vomiting.

Look for: Pills of various colors.

Drug: **Heroin, Morphine, Codeine**

Physical symptoms: Stupor, drowsiness, needle marks, watery eyes, runny nose.

Look for: Drug paraphenalia and equipment (needle, syringe, tourniquet, etc.)

Drug: **Glue (Sniffing)**

Physical symptoms: Violence, drunk appearance, dreamy or blank expression.

Look for: Tubes of glue, glue smears, handkerchiefs.

Exercise 14.1 (Continued)

DRUG AND ALCOHOL REVIEW QUIZ

Write T (True) or F (False):

_T_   1. Alcohol is a drug.

_T_   2. Mixing different types of depressant drugs greatly increases the risk of an over-dose.

_T_   3. Two marijuana cigarettes have about the same lung damage potential as a full pack of tobacco cigarettes.

_T_   4. You can become an alcoholic even if you drink nothing but beer.

_F_   5. Being the last one to pass out from use of alcohol proves you are a real man or a real woman.

_T_   6. Studies are beginning to show that marijuana is a highly dangerous drug.

_T_   7. Marijuana and alcohol are especially dangerous for drivers.

_T_   8. People can feel great without drugs.

Circle the letter or letters of the correct response.

1. Which three of the following substances do scientists agree cause the greatest number of birth and pre-birth problems?

    (a.) LSD

    (b.) Marijuana cigarettes

    (c.) Alcohol

    (d.) Tobacco cigarettes

    e. Caffeine

2. Which of the following substances have no known side effects?

    a. Aspirin

    b. Codeine

    c. Alcohol

    d. Marijuana

    e. Penicillin

Name _____

Date _____ Hour _____

3. Which of the following are healthier for your body than using drugs to feel good?

   a. Hobbies

   b. Athletics

   c. Music

   d. Working

WORD PUZZLE

Hidden in the letters in the box below are the names of 20 substances that contain drugs. Circle the words as you find them. They may be horizontal, vertical, or diagonal, forward or backward. Remember, drugs are chemical substances that cause change in the body systems. The words used in the puzzle are the following:

alcohol	cola	Pepto Bismol
Alka-Seltzer	Contac	Sominex
Anacin	Dristan	tea
aspirin	Excedrin	tobacco
beer	Listerine	Tums
Bufferin	Nyquil	wine
coffee	Nytol	

```
O  E  N  A  S  P  I  R  I  N  F  W  E
A  X  Y  N  T  M  E  Y  T  O  B  Q  P
L  C  Q  A  F  E  M  H  U  I  L  A  E
K  E  U  C  B  S  A  Y  M  A  X  L  P
A  D  I  I  G  N  W  U  S  L  S  I  T
S  R  L  N  T  O  B  A  C  C  O  S  O
E  I  D  R  I  S  T  A  N  O  M  T  B
L  N  O  K  E  D  H  P  Y  H  I  E  I
T  C  O  N  T  A  C  L  T  O  N  R  S
Z  O  I  V  L  Z  G  S  O  L  E  I  M
E  W  C  O  F  F  E  E  L  J  X  N  O
R  P  C  B  U  F  F  E  R  I  N  E  L
```

Exercise 14.2

Name _____

Date _____ Hour _____

STAGES OF ADOLESCENT CHEMICAL USE

GOALS

In this exercise you will learn

1. to look at stages of chemical use,

2. examine how others view chemical use, and

3. to check your and others' chemical use.

INTRODUCTION

Very often the road from chemical use to misuse is long and involved. Individuals just don't wake up to be suddenly addicted to chemicals. It is important not only to recognize your own level of use but that of your family and friends.

DIRECTIONS

1. Read the chart on *"Stages in Adolescent Chemical Use"* and make notes in reference to each section.

2. Participate in the discussion.

3. Fill out the sheet entitled *"Summing It Up."*

4. Develop a more comprehensive plan to change chemical use by self or others. Share with the leader.

STAGES IN ADOLESCENT CHEMICAL USE

Intake	What the World Sees
STAGE ONE, Experimental Use (Late grade school or early junior high years)	
1. Occasional beer drinking, pot-smoking or use of inhalants (glue sniffing, sniffing aerosols, etc.). Usually done on weekends or during the summer, mostly with friends.	Often unplanned, using beer sneaked from home, model glue, etc.
2. Easy to get high (low tolerance).	Little use of "harder" drugs at this stage.
3. Thrill of acting grown up and defying parents is part of the high.	

Exercise 14.2 (Continued)

Intake	What the World Sees
STAGE TWO, More Regular Use (Late junior high and early senior high years)	
4. Tolerance increases with increased use. More parties involving kegs, pot, possibly pills or hash. Acceptance of the idea that "everyone does it" and wanting to be in on it. Disdain of "local pot or 3.2 beer." Staying out later, even all night.	More money involved, false IDs used. Alcohol or pot bought and shared with friends.
	Parents become aware of use. May start a long series of "groundings" for late hours.
5. Use of wine or liquor **may** increase, but beer remains the most popular drink. Willing to suffer hangovers.	Drug-using friends often not introduced to parents.
6. Consumption increases and pride in being able to "handle it" increases.	Lying to parents about the extent of use and use of money for drugs.
7. Use on week nights begins, and school skipping may increase.	School activities are dropped, especially sports. Grades drop. Truancy increases.
8. Blackouts may begin, and talk with friends about "What did I do last night?" occurs.	Nondrug-using friends are dropped. Weekend-long parties may start.
9. Solitary use begins—even smoking at home (risk taking increases). Concentration on fooling parents or teachers when high.	
10. Preoccupation with use begins. The next high is carefully planned and anticipated. Source of supply is a matter of worry.	
11. Use during the day starts. Smoking before school to "make it through the morning." Use of "dust" may increase, or experiments with acid, speed, or barbs may continue.	
STAGE THREE, Daily Preoccupation	
12. Use of harder drug increases (speed, acid, barbs, dust).	Possible dealing or fronting for others.
13. Number of times high during the week increases. Amount of money spent for drugs increases (concealing savings withdrawals from parents).	Possible court trouble for minor consumption or possession. May be arrested for driving while intoxicated. Probation may result.

Name _____

Date _____ Hour _____

Intake	What the World Sees

STAGE THREE, . . .continued

14. "Social use" decreases—getting loaded rather than just high. Being high becomes normal.

May try to cut down or quit to convince self that there is no problem with drugs.

Most straight friends are dropped.

15. Buying more and using more—all activities seem to include drug use or alcohol.

Money owed for drugs may increase. More truancy and fights with parents about drug use.

16. Possible theft to get money to ensure a supply. There may be a contact with "bigger" dealers.

17. Solitary use increases. User will isolate self from other using friends.

18. Lying about or hiding the drug supply. Stash may be concealed from friends.

STAGE FOUR, Dependency

19. Getting high during school or at work. Difficult to face the day without drugs. Drugs are used to escape self.

Guilt feelings increase. Questioning own use but unable to control the urge.

20. Possible use of injectable drugs. Friends are burnouts (and may take pride in the label).

Low self-image and self-hate. Casual sexual involvement. Continued denial of problem.

21. Can't tell what normal behavior is any more; normal means being stoned nearly constantly.

School dropped. Dealing may increase along with police involvement. Parents may "give up."

22. Physical condition worsens. Loss of weight, more frequent illnesses, memory suffers, flashbacks may increase. Thoughts of suicide may increase.

Paranoia increases. Cost of habit increases with most money going for habit.

Loss of control over use.

Exercise 14.2 (Continued)

SUMMING IT UP

1. My use of chemicals is

    - (Experimental)

    - More regular use

    - Daily preoccupation

    - Dependency

2. The daily use of someone close to me is _____ experimental. _____

3. Plan to modify use of self or someone close to me.

Exercise 14.3

MY OWN CHEMICAL USE

GOALS

In this exercise you will learn

1. the problems involved with alcohol and marijuana, and

2. how to examine your own feelings about the effect of marijuana and alcohol.

DIRECTIONS

1. Review the material in the first few pages of Module 14.

2. Ask yourself "Do I agree with the material presented at the beginning of Module 14?"

   a. If so, proceed to item 3.

   b. If not, find reliable references resources to support your position.

3. Think of persons whom you know who use drugs and/or alcohol. Identify how the chemical(s) affects them.

4. Examine your own use of chemicals (cigarettes, tranquilizers, caffeine, alcohol, marijuana) by completing the "Exercise." If you have never used any of these chemicals but know someone who has, complete the exercise on the basis of what you believe occurred with that person.

EXERCISE

1. In regard to your first experience with mood-altering chemicals (caffeine, tobacco, alcohol, tranquilizers, marijuana, etc.)

   How old were you?

   14

   What was the situation (where used)?

   party

   How did you feel (effect of the chemical)?

   pretty good

   When was the chemical used again?

   ?

   Did you try other chemicals?

   no

   If so, what?

Exercise 14.3 (Continued)

2. What were effects of mood-altering chemicals on your life (check appropriate blanks, explain).

AREAS	PROBLEMS WITH
HOME	
Mom	
Dad	
Brother	
Sister	
SCHOOL	
Grades	
Teachers	
Administrators	
Counselors	
IN CLASS	
Concentration	
Grades	
Friends	
IN THE COMMUNITY	
Work	
Police	
Neighbors	

Name _____

Date _____ Hour _____

3. Describe other changes in your life resulting from chemicals.

> Are none.

4. Describe chemical usage of your friends.

> I have a wide variety of friends, some who use drugs a lot and some who don't at all.

5. Describe how you would like to change your life right now.

> don't want to

6. What and how much chemical substances did you have this week?

alcohol. tiny, bit

Soft drinks. 2 liter

a. What were the positive effects?

Kept me awake

b. What were the negative effects?

none at all

7. What substance and how much of it did I use this week?

same as above

a. What were its positive effects?

same as above

b. What were its negative effects?

same as above

Exercise 14.4

Name _____

Date _____ Hour _____

TWENTY THINGS I LOVE TO DO
AND MEANINGFUL RELATIONSHIPS

When attempting to free yourself of chemicals, fill your life with meaningful activities. Another important aspect to maintaining a happy, healthy life is having and maintaining good friendships. These activities and friendships need to be free of drug and alcohol abuse. How often are you really involved in activities that give you a natural high? How often do you see friends who are good for you? You will be better able to answer these questions once this exercise has been completed.

GOALS

In this exercise you will learn

1. to identify things that you have to do,

2. to examine the pattern of your activities, and

3. to examine your relationships.

DIRECTIONS

1. Fill in the left column of form entitled *"20 Things I Love To Do."*

2. As the trainer gives specific directions, fill in the other columns to classify the 20 activities you listed.

3. Discuss in the total group the results from doing the *"20 Things I Love To Do."*

4. List on the *"Assessment of Meaningful Relationships, Part I"* your most significant friends. Then assess each friend selected according to the requirements of the form.

5. Answer the questions to Part II of this exercise.

6. Discuss in the total group the results from doing the *"Assessment of Meaningful Relationships."*

20 THINGS I LOVE TO DO

1. play soccer										
2. think										
3. sleep										
4. skate (ice)										
5. be involved										
6. firehouse										
7. run										
8. watch T.V.										
9. play softball										
10. be w/ Angie										
11. help others										
12. learn										
13. travel										
14. swim										
15. exercise										
16. talk										
17. drive fast										
18. fly										
19. be w/ friends										
20.										

Name _____

Date _____   Hour _____

ASSESSMENT OF MEANINGFUL RELATIONSHIPS (PART I)

Names of Ten Friends	How Many Years Have You Known This Person?	Is the Person (M)ale or (F)emale	Enter the Initial Letter of Your Response				Rank Your Friends From 1 to 10
			(D)o or (T)alk or (B)oth?	Once a... (D)ay (W)eek (M)onth (Y)ear	You Meet (S)ocially (SCH)ool (W)ork (F)amily	Meet, Which Do You Do? (I)nitiate (R)espond (B)oth	
1. Dave B.	7	M	B	D	S, Sch	B	1
2. Dave Peck	4	M	B	D	S, Sch	B	6
3. Mike Chester	8	M	B	D	"	B	8
4. Mike Vincent	4	M	B	D	"	B	10
5. Chad Fitzwater	5	M	B	D	"	B	4
6. Angie Forrester	1	F	B	D	"	B	7
7. Missy Knapp	1	F	B	D	"	B	5
8. Kenya Mathews	1	F	B	D	"	B	9
9. Charity Bedell	7	F	B	D	"	B	2
10. Jeff Rozelle	9	M	B	D	"	B	3

Exercise 14.4 (Continued)

ASSESSMENT OF MEANINGFUL RELATIONSHIPS, PART II

Analyze the information you recorded in the "Assessment of Meaningful Relationships" form.

1. What did you discover about yourself in terms of your relationships with your significant friends?

    Basicly the same

2. How wide is the span of activities represented?

    wide

3. How often are you really involved in activities that give you a natural high?

    daily

4. How many of the relationships involve spending time with or are dependent upon chemicals?

    O

5. To what extent do these 10 friends

    a. support your need for chemical dependency?

    don't

    b. support your needs so that you remain free from chemical dependency?

    all

6. How often do you see friends who are good for you?

    every day

7. How do you think activities and meaningful relationships contribute to or prevent the need for chemical dependency?

    they contribute to prevention of chemical dependency

Exercise 14.5

PERSONAL INVENTORY

Take a few minutes to look at yourself in terms of your own life-style and the life-styles of others around you. It also is important to understand that there are some positive areas in your life and to recognize what these areas are.

GOALS

In this exercise you will learn

1. to look at alternative highs, and

2. to suggest alternative highs for others.

DIRECTIONS

1. Complete the Pencil/Paper Exercises Numbers 1 and 2. Your instructor will guide you.

2. Discuss the results.

PENCIL/PAPER EXERCISE NUMBER 1

How do you get high? (Not just drugs and alcohol)

Below are ways to have natural highs. Brainstorm other ways and add to the list. Then circle two ways that best work for you. Write an explanation of how and/or why these work for you.

1. Physical feats — get rid of stress, physical high

2. Projects

3. Recognition

4. Hobbies

5. Sex

6. Flirtations

7. Giving gifts or services — makes me feel good inside

8. Animals

9. Out of doors

10. Others (You list . . .)

Exercise 14.5 (Continued)

PENCIL/PAPER EXERCISE NUMBER 2

Stereotypes. Below are listed a few stereotypes. Add to the list. Then circle any of the stereotypes into which you fit or did fit. Do you want to change? Will any of the ones listed in Exercise Number 1 be of assistance in helping you change? If so, which ones and how?

1. Druggie

2. Pothead

3. Heroin addict

4. Coker

5. Duster

6. Juicer

7. Sporto   I like this combination just as long as it doesn't get to my head.

8. Preppie

9. Goodie-goodie

10. Others (You list...)

Exercise 14.6

RECOGNIZING PROBLEMS IN OTHERS

GOALS

In this exercise you will learn

1. to look at how the abusive behavior affects you, and

2. to help you sort out your feelings and action.

INTRODUCTION

As you become more and more concerned about friends who are abusing drugs and alcohol, you may decide to try to confront them with the problem, but it is first good to examine how it affects you and your feelings that have developed.

DIRECTIONS

1. Keep a journal of things that have been happening when you are with your friend(s). Use the chart, *"Journal of Happenings,"* for this purpose.

2. Try to develop a plan of action to confront your friend or family member.

3. Continue over a period of time with the chart.

JOURNAL OF HAPPENINGS

Date	Behavior of Others	My Feelings	My Reaction	What I Would Like to See Done

Exercise 14.7

Name _____

Date _____ Hour _____

PUTTING CONFRONTATION INTO ACTION

In Module 11 you learned some confrontation skills. Please think about how this could be used with someone you know in terms of intervention.

WHAT IS INTERVENTION?

In an intervention you join forces with others to confront an individual with the realities of the illness in an honest and supportive way. A meeting is arranged in which you and others tell the individual how they behaved while drinking or under the influence of mood-altering drugs and describe the harm and hurt each of you felt. In this manner, the addicted person sees the effects of the disease from the perspective of friends and loved ones.

Friends and family may wish to participate in an intervention. It is a good idea to have a professional counselor available to facilitate the intervention.

The actual intervention must be done with concern, respect, and love rather than condemnation. This allows the dependent person to remain open to the information presented and not become defensive or unreceptive.

An intervention, if carefully prepared for, most often motivates the person whom you care about to seek professional treatment.

GOALS

In this exercise you will learn

1. to role play a confrontation of a friend concerning drug use, and

2. to discuss skills and consequences.

DIRECTIONS

1. Divide into clusters of three.

2. Have one person as the confronter, another the facilitator (a professional counselor), and the other person as the one with the problem.

3. Choose one of the situations given by your trainer or one with which a member of the cluster is familiar.

Module 14   Drugs and Alcohol Abuse—Intervention and Prevention   31

4. Role play the situation in which the confronter and facilitator confront the person with the problem. Confront with concern, respect, and love.

5. Following role playing, share with each other the feeling during the role play.

6. If time permits, exchange roles and repeat Directions 3, 4, and 5 until each has portrayed all three roles.

Exercise 14.8

FAMILIES AFFECTED BY ALCOHOLISM

GOALS

In this exercise you will learn

1. the impact on family members of alcoholism,

2. the roles that family members play, and

3. how to get help for yourself.

INTRODUCTION

Often the abusers themselves are not the ones who suffer. Additional family members are affected, sometimes for a lifetime. Often within the family, a co-alcoholic or an enabler is the one who perpetuates the abuse problem. In the last several years, support groups have been growing by leaps and bounds, for example, Al-Anon, Alateen, and Adult Children of Alcoholics, that have helped family members cope through learning the 12-step approach. This exercise will help you to examine your own family and their addictive behavior in reference to alcohol and the role that you might play. You also will begin to understand your potential for alcoholism.

DIRECTIONS

1. Read the information concerning *"Alcoholism—A Family Disease."*

2. Examine the various roles within the family.

3. Decide if you fit into any of these roles.

4. Review the information in the Chart entitled *"Social Drinkers and Alcoholics' Body Reaction to Alcohol."*

5. After you have examined the different roles in the family of alcoholics, ask yourself if you fit into any of these roles. How do you know?

6. If you or someone you know could be assisted by external help, contact a community organization such as Al-Anon, Alateen, or Adult Children of Alcoholics.

ALCOHOLISM—A FAMILY DISEASE

Did You Know?

- One out of eight drinkers becomes an alcoholic,

- One out of four children has one or more parents who are alcoholics.

The evidence supports the statement that many individuals are infected by the disease of alcoholism.

Co-Dependency

Within the family of an alcoholic, most often a co-alcoholic or enabler also is present. This is a person or persons who have the same behaviors and feelings and are preoccupied with the alcoholic's behavior. Enablers' focus is on controlling alcoholics' intake of alcohol as well as their behavior while drinking. They provide the support system for the alcoholism to progress. The enabler may be a spouse, friend, employer, parent, or child. Enablers seem to have no choice in what they do. Just as alcoholics lose their ability to choose not to have a second drink after the first, enablers seem to have no choice in how they behave and feel.

As the abuser and enabler get more out of control, others within the family take on the responsibilities of the neglected family. The children are affected not only by the abuser and the enabler but also by the chaos and abnormal family dynamics created by the preoccupation with alcoholism.

Some of the characteristics of co-dependency are as follows:

1. My good feelings about who I am stem from being liked by you.

2. My good feelings about who I am stem from receiving approval from you.

3. My self-esteem is bolstered by relieving your pain.

4. I need to be needed.

5. I'm critical, and then I feel guilty.

6. Your clothing and personal appearance is dictated by my desires because I feel you are a reflection of me.

7. I believe that I can fix it up, always failing and feeling depressed.

What Does The Alcoholic Home Look Like?

On the surface it looks fine but, underneath, the alcoholic and the enabler are so involved with the disease that they are not available physically and/or emotionally to the role normally fulfilled by that person within the family, i.e., mother, father, child. Often unpredictable and inconsistent behavior occurs. Some embarrassment is associated with what is going on at home. Some of the family rules are

> don't think,
> don't feel,
> don't talk,
> don't be,
> don't get angry,
> don't trust,
> don't count on things,
> don't say "No,"
> don't be honest, and
> don't ask for help.

These are sometimes implied, sometimes explicitly stated. These rules come about because of the chaos, unpredictability, and inconsistency of the family system.

Exercise 14.8 (Continued)

Roles That Family Members Take

Individuals survive the alcoholic family in many ways. Often the children take on various roles. These roles were described by Wegscheider and Black (1981, 1982).

- **Heroes.** The overly responsible children who learn that they cannot control the alcoholic's drinking or the enabler parent's response to the drinker. These heroes learn that they can control the environment, for example, taking care of siblings, laundry, schedules.

  As adults, the heroes become overly responsible. They often do not learn how to give and take or to relax, and frequently a lot of tension and separation from others occurs.

- **Scapegoats.** This is just opposite of the heroes. They are angry, and their anger results from their inability to deal with the family chaos. Scapegoats have problems following rules. Often they react negatively to authority figures. Because of their anger, they may begin stealing, lying, taking drugs, or running away in an effort to express the anger. They usually do poorly in school.

  Scapegoats as adults often cannot develop commitments in relationships. They often end up in hassles with the law. They continue to take excessive risks and may have drinking problems.

- **Lost Child, or Adjuster.** These children merely adjust to whatever is happening. Their self-esteem, or identity, is to cause no trouble. Their common belief is that they can't do anything about it anyway, so why try? Their primary feelings are loneliness and fear of abandonment.

  Lost children become adjusting adults. They may find that the easiest procedure is to avoid positions where a need exists or may occur to take control and make decisions. They have not learned to stand up for themselves, lead, or initiate. For them to establish relationships may be tremendously difficult and when they do they may be very chaotic.

- **Caretakers.** Children who derive their identity from listening to their family's problems in the hope of making the family well are caretakers. They often feel lonely and depressed. They never consider their own needs. They are little social workers, always ready to help others as a means of avoiding their loneliness.

  Caretaking children often become placating adults. Caretakers experience excessive dependency on others. They feel depressed and lonely. Caretakers are often employed in helping professions.

- **Mascots.** Mascots are usually the last of the children. Mascots are the most deprived at home because the family has already adapted to chaos, unpredictability, and inconsistency. Normally well liked by the parents, mascots are enjoyed for their sense of humor. Sometimes they seem hyperactive. They are often poor learners with limited mental development. Their predominant feeling is fear.

  Mascots become exceedingly forceful adults. They do not understand how to deal with tension and its related feelings. Stress-related illnesses surface, and many fears develop into phobias. They often have difficulty acquiring and maintaining employment and establishing commitments in a relationship.

Exercise 14.8 (Continued)

CUES THAT INDICATE A TEENAGER MAY BE HAVING DIFFICULTY BECAUSE OF PARENTAL ALCOHOLISM

1. Avoidance or difficulty talking about family and feelings.

   Example: The helpee may change the subject or remain silent when drinking is discussed.

2. Rationalization of parents' behavior.

   Example: A helpee states, "I feel so sorry for Mom. She can't do anything about what's happening."

3. Identification of their own drinking patterns.

   Example: Bragging about their own drinking, excessive mention of partying.

SOCIAL DRINKERS AND ALCOHOLICS' BODY REACTION TO ALCOHOL

Recent research indicates that our bodies react differently when we are social drinkers than when we are alcoholics. The following is a chart that indicates the difference.

How alcohol is processed in the body of a SOCIAL DRINKER

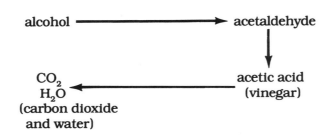

How alcohol is processed in the body of the ALCOHOLIC

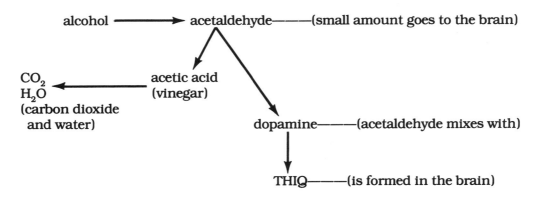

THIQ—Tetra Hydro Iso Quinoline. The latest scientific evidence shows that this remains in the brain indefinitely!

EXERCISE 14.9

JUST SAY "NO"

GOALS

In this exercise, you will learn

1. about peer pressure,

2. negative consequences of alcohol use,

3. positive consequences of nonuse, and

4. learn to say "No" in a party situation.

INTRODUCTION

While individuals are attending social gatherings, a frequent thing to do is drink. Generally alcohol can be easily obtained, and peer pressure to drink is often part of the party setting. To abstain or to use in moderation has some positive consequences while misuse, abuse, and dependence has some negative consequences.

DIRECTIONS

1. Participate in the discussion using the *"Questions to be Discussed."*

2. Role play a party scene and learn to say "No."

3. Write about how it felt to say "No."

QUESTIONS TO BE DISCUSSED

1. What is peer pressure?
   when friends force you to do something you normally wouldn't do

2. Based on early learning in this module, what is the difference among use, moderate use, abuse, and dependency?
   the amount of alcohol consumed in a certain amount of time

3. What are some positive consequences of nonuse?
   you will always have a clear mind, full reflexes

4. What are some negative consequences of use and abuse?
   slowed reflexes, loss of friends

5. Divide into groups of three. All of the members should role play the person being pressured:

   Scene: All of the individuals at the party are drinking and smoking pot. Most of the group are your friends, and they are trying to get you to drink with them. You are saying "No" gently and firmly.

Exercise 14.9 (Continued)

6. Discussion

- What are some consequences for saying no?

  you might lose some "friends"

- What are some consequences for giving into the peer pressure?

  get yourself into trouble

SELECTED REFERENCES TO WRITE
TO FOR FURTHER INFORMATION

AL-ANON FAMILY GROUP HEADQUARTERS
Post Office Box 142
Madison Square Station
New York, New York 10010

ALCOHOLICS ANONYMOUS WORLD SERVICE INC.
Post Office Box 459
Grand Central Station
New York, New York 10017

COMP-CARE PUBLICATION
2415 Annapolis Lane, Suite 140
Minneapolis, Minnesota 55441

HAZELDEN LITERATURE DEPARTMENT
Post Office Box 176
Center City, Minnesota 55012

JOHNSON INSTITUTE
10700 Olson Memorial Highway
Minneapolis, Minnesota 55441-6199

NATIONAL COUNCIL ON ALCOHOLISM
733 Third Avenue
New York, New York 10017

MODULE XV

STRESS MANAGEMENT—
MANAGEMENT
MOVING TOWARD
WELLNESS

MODULE **15**

STRESS MANAGEMENT— MOVING TOWARD WELLNESS

Today we are becoming increasingly aware of discomforts and dangers of chronic tension. We are bombarded with statistics that indicate that infectious diseases have been replaced by stress-related diseases, which have become the leading cause of illness in today's society. We have come to understand that stress is often very expensive. Illness directly attributable to stress has a cost figure for industry in excess of $2.8 billion in lost workdays. Of all medical expenses paid by Americans, 70% are for stress-related disorders.

Numerous stress warning signals are present that we experience every day, for example, feeling unable to slow down and relax, exploding in anger in response to a minor irritation, experiencing anxiety or tension that lasts for more than a few days, feeling that things frequently go wrong, being unable to focus attention, and having frequent or prolonged feelings of boredom. Often stress is disguised as fatigue, sexual problems, sleep disturbances, tension or migraine headaches, cold hands or feet, aching neck and shoulder muscles, indigestion, menstrual distress, nausea or vomiting, loss of appetite, diarrhea, and ulcers. Physical symptoms that often accompany stress are heart palpitations, constipation, lower back pain, allergy or asthma attacks, shortness of breath, frequent colds, frequent low-grade infections, and frequent minor accidents. These stress-related symptoms lead us into other problems such as increased consumption of alcohol or increased dependence on drugs.

Some of the sources of stress in teenagers are sexual maturation through development, social issues or problems, physical size, shyness or the inability to meet people, health, money, competition, burnout from too many activities, self-concept problems, drug-related pressures and problems, and school pressure or problems, parental pressure, interference, inattention, or discipline problems. All of these and many more lead to physical and psychological stress problems.

Now that we are more attuned to stress in our lives, we make conscious efforts to relax. We often subscribe to stress management programs and self-help groups. Stress itself, however, is not the culprit. Stress is what has kept the whole human race functioning since the beginning. Some stressors are necessary, even desirable, and are called excitement or challenges. Without them, life would be dull. Our problem then becomes not stress but how we approach and manage stress. *Managed stress makes us productive and happy people;* mismanaged stress can be harmful.

Our manifestation of how our personalities cope with the environment is our ability or inability to process stress in our life. While stress is but one indicator of the impact of the mental on the physical and vice versa, a direct, verifiable correlation exists between our physical and mental health and our lifestyles and general outlook on life.

How we approach situations is very important. Some of us approach situations in a stressed manner, which of course leads to problems. Friedman and Roseman refer to Type A and Type B personalities. *Type A* personalities are the more hurried, the more time-conscious, striving to excel, and more prone to heart problems. *Type B* personalities are the more relaxed, easygoing individuals.

Our present epidemic of stress and its resulting psychophysical ailments is the result of our misunderstanding of stress. Obviously, what is needed is a solid, intelligent approach to stress management.

The best way to manage stress is to look at our approach to stress and how we live. Do we have healthy lifestyles? Are we moving toward wellness?

Health professionals are coming to the realization that morbidity and mortality rates of Americans are related to chronic disorders, largely brought on by lifestyle (what we choose to eat and drink and the nature of our environment).

Statistics show that infectious diseases have been replaced by cardiovascular diseases, respiratory illness, stress disorders, cancer, and other lifestyle related ailments. Most health problems that plague Americans today are ultimately not health problems at all—they are behavior problems requiring the alteration of characteristic response patterns.

A known authority on health thinks that four measures are consistently signaled as central to preventive medicine (Pelletier, 1979):

1. status of health,
2. change in lifestyle,
3. management of stress, and
4. diet and exercise.

In a pioneer study of adults, researchers discovered that both the level of health and the life expectancy are related to seven health practices:

1. sleeping adequate periods,
2. maintaining close-to-ideal weight,
3. not smoking,
4. taking no more than two alcoholic drinks at a time,
5. exercising regularly,
6. eating breakfast, and
7. not eating between meals.

These investigators found that the effects of these habits were additive, that 45-year-old adults who adapted all 7 practices as part of their lifestyle could expect to live 7 to 11 years longer than those ignoring all or part of these factors (Belloc & Breslow, 1972).

The issue of an ever-growing sedentary population is also worthy of note. Recent studies indicate that a person with a sedentary job, when hospitalized, will have a length of stay that is 54 percent longer than a person who is actively engaged in some type of exercise on the job. Exercise can contribute to the total wellness of the individual in numerous ways. It is associated with healthier bodies, reduced cardio-vascular problems, and lower back pain; it also is responsible for lessening depressions, effecting a faster recovery rate in illness, promoting a better sense of well-being, and leading to effective management of stress and improved psychological variables (such as perception of one's body). In discussing the effects of our mental outlook on our physical well-being, the exercise component cannot be neglected.

The simplest definition of wellness and health is the optimum condition of physical and mental well-being. In examining our ability to lead a happy life, an important procedure also is to examine the level of coping, stress, and personality. Learning to lead a healthy life means having that life in balance—balancing the physical, mental, emotional, spiritual, and nutritional parts of the individual.

Use. This module could be taught separately or it could be placed early in the training. It is appropriate for high school and older adults. The module is not designed to be a complete program in stress management and wellness. It simply helps us to become aware of our own stress and stressors and suggests different approaches to coping with problems. If you decide to work on this area, the suggestion is that you become involved in a program of lifestyle change that lasts at least 12 weeks, ideally 6 months.

Belloc, N.B. & Breslow, H. (1972). Relationship of physical health states and health practice. *Preventive Medicine, I*, 409-421.

Name _____

Date _____ Hour _____

WHAT HAPPENS UNDER STRESS?

To understand what happens to you during stress is very important.

GOALS

In this exercise you will learn

1. to understand stress, and

2. to identify events that cause the most stress in your life.

DIRECTIONS

1. Read the introductory material to Module 15 on stress and activity.

2. Discuss with your trainer any questions you may have concerning the issue.

3. Use the "Personal Stressors Appraisal Form" to help identify stressors.

4. Discuss your responses in the group.

PERSONAL STRESSORS APPRAISAL FORM

1. List the ten events (on the line to the right) that cause the most stress in your life.

a. ___S___ _____term papers_____

b. ___H, B___ _____my brother_____

c. ___H, P___ _____my parents_____

d. ___S___ _____exams_____

e. ___S___ _____certain history teachers_____

f. ___F___ _____some friends_____

g. ___H, J, W___ _____too many activities_____

h. ___*___ _____daily decisions_____

i. _____ _____

j. _____ _____

2. Place all appropriate letters or symbols from the following table on the line to the left of each event listed.

       H   Occurs in the home.

       S   Occurs at school.

      W   Occurs at work.

       *   Occurred this week.

       $ Involves money.

       P   Includes participation of a parent.

       B   Includes participation of a brother or sister.

       F   Includes participation of a friend.

3. Answer the following questions.

    a. What kind of circumstances tend to surround your most stressful events?

        Basicly, all of my stress surrounds on my wanting to be active in too many things and not having enough time for them

    b. Has this been a stressful event in your life for a long period of time?

        Not really, most of this started this year

    c. Do your parents have the same stressful events in their lives? Are any of these events a part of the process of growing and maturing?

        I don't think so. They probably are because it is teaching me responsibility and time management.

Exercise 15.2

EFFECTS OF STRESS ON ME

Examine and understand the effects of stress in both a positive and a negative manner. Also important is for you to know how stress affects you—mentally, emotionally, and physically. If you recognize stress signals, then you can begin working on your stress.

GOALS

In this exercise you will learn

1. to understand how stress affects you, and

2. to recognize stress.

DIRECTIONS

1. Look at and study the section entitled *"Danger Signals of Stress."*

2. Read the material entitled *"The Alarm Reaction," "Adaptation,"* and *"Breakdown."*

3. Gain a working understanding of the material on negative and positive results of stress by studying the material entitled *"Negative Results of Stress"* and *"Positive Results of Stress."*

4. Think about how stress affects you in both positive and negative manners and write how you believe stress may affect you by completing the *"Effects of Stress Form."*

5. Discuss in the group the concepts generated from this Exercise.

DANGER SIGNALS OF STRESS

1. You become nauseated during a crisis.

2. You are chronically tired with no great physical exertion to account for it.

3. You catch yourself gritting your teeth, clamping your jaw, or tightening your lips.

4. You are plagued by indecision and have a substantial amount of unfinished work piled up because you cannot decide where to begin.

5. You become furious at inanimate objects—a missing pen, a letter, or a car that won't start immediately.

6. You habitually sit stiffly on the edge of your chair or hold a steering wheel in an iron grip.

7. You have developed nervous habits such as finger tapping, nail biting, or jerky movements.

8. You increasingly reach for a tranquilizer or an alcoholic brace.

9. You show irritation over petty things or feel neglected or left out.

10. Your palms are sweaty, your stomach hurts, your head aches.

Simply put, stress is a biological or psychological disruption. Hans Selye, an authority on stress, defined "stress" as the nonspecific response to any demand. In everyday terms you can think of your personal stress as your body's mental, emotional, and physical reaction to forces that impact on you. These are situations that cause you to experience fear, elation, anger, excitation, boredom, confusion, or anxiety. The circumstances surrounding such reactions may be happy or unhappy, good or bad. For example, a new job can be either good or bad, a new friend can either be good or bad. It depends on how we react to stress.

THE ALARM REACTION

What happens when we react to stress?

The first thing that happens when you perceive or imagine a threatening situation is that your biological alarms go off. Your nervous system sends impulses to the hypothalamus gland in your brain, which in turn sends a message to your pituitary and adrenal glands. This mobilizes all of your body's action systems. It's like sounding action stations on a battleship. The hormones entering your blood stream cause heart and respiration rates to speed up. Blood pressure elevates and extra supplies of blood become available to your muscles. Your body is poised for action. This is what is called the "fight or flight" response because it prepares you for whatever is necessary for survival.

Fortunately, most of the stressful situations you face in your life, job, or family are not life-threatening; but your body does not know that. Thus, you may find yourself continually in a state of emotional arousal because of the stressful events occurring around you.

ADAPTATION

When you are subjected to a stressor (stressful situation or event) you must make some kind of adjustment or "adaptation." You have to accommodate yourself to the new set of conditions occasioned by the stressor. A change in schools, job, or family financial situation are typical examples.

The ability to do this depends on our storehouse of adaptive energy. The person who is always in a stressful state, who does not know what to do about stress, who makes no effective effort to resolve the stress, eventually depletes the available supply of adaptive energy.

Exercise 15.2 (Continued)

BREAKDOWN

"Breakdown" or exhaustion occurs when you can no longer continue in high gear. The mechanism breaks down. You get sick. Not everyone reacts to unresolved stress in the same way—some people experience high blood pressure; some, gastrointestinal disorders; others, coronary artery disease. Stress has many possible negative effects, but if it is handled in a positive manner, a healthier person may emerge.

NEGATIVE RESULTS OF STRESS

Mental	Emotional	Physical
Worry	Irritability	Low energy level
Poor concentration	Mood swings	Poor physical condition
Memory loss	Disruption of body (sleeping, eating)	Aches and pains
Lowered self-image	Depression	Headaches
Poor time management	Anxiety	Neck pain
	Frustration	Low back pain
	Tension	Grinding teeth
		Insomnia
		Low resistance to colds

POSITIVE RESULTS OF STRESS

Mental	Emotional	Physical
Enhanced creativity	Sense of control	High energy level
Enhanced thinking	Responsive to environment	Stamina
Becoming goal oriented	Improved morale	Endurance
Decisiveness	Improved interpersonal relations	Flexibility
		Freedom from stress

Name _____

Date _____ Hour _____

EFFECTS OF STRESS FORM

Fill in examples of how you believe stress may affect you:

Positively

Mental ____ Becoming goal oriented _____

Emotional ____ Improved interpersonal relationship _____

Physical ____ High Energy level _____

Negatively

Mental ____ poor concentration _____

Emotional ____ frustration _____

Physical ____ low resistance to colds _____

Exercise 15.3

Name _____

Date _____ Hour _____

COPING WITH STRESSORS

An important step in being able to handle stress in the future is to recognize what techniques you are now using to cope with stress.

GOALS

In this exercise you will learn

1. to recognize how you cope with stress with effective and ineffective techniques, and

2. to list techniques that work for you.

DIRECTIONS

1. In the *"Coping With Stress Form"* provided on the next page, list four of your major stressors identified in Exercise 15.1. Examples are provided to help you start.

2. List your stress reactions to each of your four major stressors.

3. List some negative effects and some positive effects of those stressors similar to the way you identified positive and negative effects in Exercise 15.2.

4. List ineffective techniques for coping with your stressors.

5. List some effective techniques you might try for coping with your stressors.

6. Divide into clusters of two and work with your partner to help each other analyze your stressors and identify effective techniques for coping with stressors.

7. Share with the total group techniques that might work for you in coping with stressors.

Exercise 15.3 (Continued)

Stressors	**Stress Reaction**
1. Fight with my mother.	1. Yell and get a headache.
2. Low grade in English	2. Depressed and can't eat; stomach hurts.
3. In trouble with boss	3. Stiff neck, anxious.

Ineffective techniques for coping with stressors:

1. Drinking.

2. Yelling.

3. Hiding in my room.

4. Keeping things inside self.

Effective techniques for coping with stressors:

1. Being assertive with boss.

2. Changing thinking about mother.

3. Identify different goals for studying.

4. Doing relaxation exercises.

My Stressors   **My Stress Reactions**

Identified in Exercise 15.1

1. _too many activities_   1. _poor time management_

2. _brother_   2. _Irritability_

3. _parents_   3. _mood swings, headaches_

4. _exams_   4. _worry, low energy level_

Exercise 15.3 (Continued)

Name _____

Date _____ Hour _____

Negative effects of my stressors and my reactions to them.

1. _I try to plan my day out better, thinking of what has to be accomplished and if I have enough time_

2. _Usually, my irritability and my frustration get the best of me and I end up hurting him_

3. _Try to avoid them and talk to them as little as possible_

4. _Try to cram all the information in my head a day or two ahead of time._

Positive effects of my stressors and my reactions to them.

1. _Helps me learn effective ways of planning my time and ways to avoid stress_

2. _Helps me to learn to control my temper and direct my anger in other ways_

3. _?_

4. _Helps me to learn better study habits and how to prepare ahead of time_

Ineffective techniques I use for coping with my stressors.

1. _____
   _____
   _____
   _____

2. _____
   _____
   _____
   _____

3. _____
   _____
   _____
   _____

4. _____
   _____
   _____
   _____

Effective techniques that I might try for coping with my stressors.

1. _____
   _____
   _____
   _____

2. _____
   _____
   _____
   _____

3. _____
   _____
   _____
   _____

4. _____
   _____
   _____
   _____

Name _____

Date _____ Hour _____

UNDERSTANDING THE DIFFERENCE BETWEEN
TENSION AND RELAXATION THROUGH IMAGERY

GOALS

In this exercise you will identify

1. how your body reacts to tension, and

2. how your body feels when relaxed.

INTRODUCTION

Before we can cope with tension, we have to be able to recognize when we are under tension. If we are tense and do not realize it, we may mope and become withdrawn or snap at others around us, addressing our tension in a negative way. Our behavior can increase our feelings of tensions and create a vicious circle of stress that helps no one. Some of us may harbor feelings inside and develop ulcers or nervous conditions and not even know why. To learn to cope with stress and tension, we must first learn to recognize within ourselves when we are under tension. From there, we need to learn techniques for coping with tension and for avoiding situations that increase our tension level.

The exercises that follow are designed to give you information about yourself and how you react to tension.

DIRECTIONS

1. Get very comfortable in a chair or lie on the floor. Make sure that your surroundings are very quiet and that no talking is occurring.

2. Listen to your trainer take you through an imagery experience.

3. In the space entitled *"Image of My Body Under Tension"* draw a picture of your body as it is feeling tense and answer the questions.

4. In the space entitled *"Image of My Body While Relaxed"* draw a picture of your body as it is feeling relaxed and answer the questions.

5. Respond to the following questions about the image.

   (a) Define tension and relaxation.

   (b) When in your daily lives have you felt tense?

   (c) When and where did you feel relaxed?

Exercise 15.4 (Continued)

(d) Are there ways to avoid feeling tense?

Example: Late to class

(e) How can we use our image experience to feel relaxed at all times?

6. In the future, refer to your relaxed image several times when you feel tense.

Exercise 15.4 (Continued)

Name _____

Date _____ Hour _____

**IMAGE OF MY BODY
UNDER TENSION**

How strong was the image?

—— Very strong

—— Moderately strong

—— Weak

How does this image fit into my daily life?

How does tension affect my body, my mind?

IMAGE OF MY BODY
WHILE RELAXED

How strong was the image?   ___   Very strong

                                   ___   Moderately strong

                                   ___   Weak

How does this image fit into my daily life?

How does being relaxed affect my body, my mind?

Exercise 15.5   Name _____

                                     Date _____ Hour _____

BALANCED HEALTHY LIFE

Think about your life. Is it in balance? Decide what part, if any, of your life is out of balance and then begin to move toward a healthier lifestyle.

GOALS

In this exercise you will learn

1. to think about the way you live and examine any parts that are out of balance, and

2. to set goals to begin a healthier lifestyle.

DIRECTIONS

1. Look at the diagram in Figure 15.1 and identify what part of your life is out of balance if any. Do so by asking yourself questions appropriate to each area to determine whether or not that area is in balance or too much or too little.

2. Set a goal to begin changing any part that may be out of balance.

3. Record your goal in the space entitled *"My Goal."*

4. Interact with another trainee and assist each other in outlining strategies for achieving your goal.

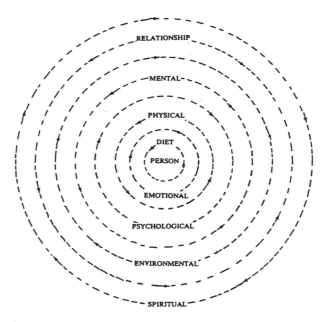

Figure 15.1. Parts essential for a balanced healthy life.

Exercise 15.5 (Continued)

MY GOAL

Record a goal you have for the next seven days. Have your goal to be associated with only one area. Try to work only one area at a time at first.

In writing your goal include, as was done in the following example, the stressor, the stressor reaction and effect on you, and the goal you have set in terms of potentially effective techniques for coping with your stressor.

Example

I have been fighting with my mother. It has caused me to be emotionally out of balance and my head hurts. For the next week I am going to talk with, not yell at, my mother and try to do some relaxation exercises.

I've been constantly fighting with my brother for the past couple of years. It seems everything he does is to annoy me. It gives me headaches and I feel frustrated. This next week I will try to control myself and get along better

Exercise 15.6

HEALTH HABITS AS A MEANS
OF REDUCING STRESS

GOALS

In this exercise you will identify areas in your life

1. that are not healthy, and

2. that you may want to change.

INTRODUCTION

The way we live has a lot to do with how we manage stress. We can control much of life by correcting a few simple habits. In this exercise is a *"Health Habits Checklist"* for use in examining some of your daily habits.

DIRECTIONS

1. Answer the questions on the *"Health Habits Checklist."*

2. Decide how you can learn about each one.

3. Decide how you can make a change in your life in terms of specific areas with which you are not satisfied.

4. Develop a plan to change some of your life-style.

Exercise 15.6 (Continued)

HEALTH HABITS CHECKLIST

	True	False
1. I do not smoke cigarettes.	✓	
2. I do not drink more than two alcoholic drinks a day.	✓	
3. I eat breakfast regularly.		✓
4. I do not eat between meals.		✓
5. I maintain normal weight.	✓	
6. I avoid caffeine and sugar.		✓
7. I exercise at least three times a week.	✓	
8. I sleep seven or eight hours a night.		✓
9. I have a good support system i.e., family and friends.	✓	
10. I wear a seat belt when riding in moving vehicles.	✓	

What areas do I need to examine?

Eating breakfast, Avoiding caffein + sugar, getting more sleep

How can I make a change in my life to be healthier?

Better eating habits, structure time better

What kind of support do I need and from whom or what?

don't need any

Exercise 15.7

Name _____

Date _____ Hour _____

THOUGHTS, FEELINGS, BEHAVIOR

GOALS

In this exercise you will learn

1. to understand the differences among thoughts, feelings, and behavior;

2. to understand how our thoughts affect our feelings, behavior; and

3. to practice changing some of my thought patterns.

INTRODUCTION

Our thoughts and feelings often affect our behavior. They work together to create stress or to relieve stress.

Thoughts. We use our brains to think. We are always thinking. When we think, often times we actually talk to ourselves. Our thoughts are our opinions, conclusions, what we understand, and about which we have experiences. Thoughts are private.

Feelings. Our emotions—whether mad, sad, glad, afraid, or ashamed—are our feelings, and they are separate from our thoughts. All of our feelings derive from our thoughts. A common mistake in sharing and expressing feelings is to say, "I feel _____" and then share a thought. Example: "I feel like today is a nice day" is a thought rather than a feeling. "Happy" is a feeling. A correct way to share a feeling is to say, "I feel happy that today is a nice day." Feelings are also private unless we choose to share them.

Behavior. What we do, what we say, or what others can see are our actions.

Our thoughts, feelings, and behavior all work together. Many times the process of thoughts, feelings, and behavior react together so fast that we forget that they are all separate. Example: A boy is walking down the street, and he sees a large dog running toward him. Immediately he starts running to his house. This happens fast. His thoughts are "That dog looks mean!" His feelings are scared, afraid, panicked. His behavior is running to the house. He could choose other alternatives if his thoughts were different.

DIRECTIONS

1. Role play the following situations with different thoughts.

   a. Your father comes home from work and says that your family is moving.

   b. You are at home alone at night, and you hear a strange noise.

   c. Your dog chews up your favorite pair of shoes.

2. Write out the following:

Thoughts	Feelings	Behavior
Alternative Thoughts	Alternative Feelings	Alternative Behavior

3. Complete the following entitled, *"Thoughts, Feelings, and Behavior."* Think about a time that you had strong feelings and what your thoughts and behavior were. How could you have changed your thoughts?

THOUGHTS, FEELINGS, AND BEHAVIOR

Think about a time that you had strong feelings and what your thoughts and behavior were. These three parts, we all have. All three parts work together. Can you think of a time that you felt really mad, sad, glad, afraid, or ashamed? Try to separate your thoughts, feelings, and actions. (Remember: We are always responsible for our own actions!)

a. Write in a few words what would help you identify a time that you had a strong feeling!

b. What were your thoughts?

c. What were your feelings?

d. What were your actions (what you did)?

4. During the day, as you have strong feelings and thoughts, write them down and consider alternative thoughts and feelings.

5. Role-play two situations that demonstrate alternative ways of thinking, feeling, and behavior.

Exercise 15.8

EXAMINING YOUR SUPPORT SYSTEM

GOALS

In this exercise you will learn

1. to understand the need for friends and family (support system),

2. to examine the level of your support system, and

3. to look at ways to expand your support system.

INTRODUCTION

Research indicates that individuals live longer if they have friends and a good support system. Daily living is much easier when we know that we can count on support from others. This is true of all of us no matter how strong or independent we are. People need people. Having a reliable support system serves as a stress buffer and reliever for us in our various roles in which we are involved, for example, with our family or in our work, school, or play. Some individuals need more social support than do others, but we all need contact at various times.

DIRECTIONS

1. Review the material developed in the previous exercise.

2. Make a list of individuals whom you need and like to have around you. No one is self-sufficient since we all depend on others for certain things. Record your list on the left side of the paper. Beside each name, indicate those things for which you can count on that person, why you have contact with that person, and why you need that person.

Name	Why Need
Dave	talk to
Angie	
Jason	
Josh	

3. Review your list and answer the following questions:

   a. How is contact made with the individuals on your list?

   b. How often do you contact them? *see them daily, at school and home*

   c. Who initiates the contact? *every day*
   both parties

4. See if individuals from your first list could be placed on the chart entitled *"Your Needs and Your Support System."* Then identify other possible persons for that list.

5. Brainstorm for possible ways to expand and or improve your support system so that your needs do not go unmet.

6. Think about how you can make more opportunities for others.

Exercise 15.8 (Continued)

YOUR NEEDS AND YOUR SUPPORT SYSTEM

Type Needed	SUPPORT SYSTEM	
	Work/School	Personal Life
Listener	Present	Present
	Possible	Possible
Belonging	Present	Present
	Possible	Possible
Has confidence in me	Present	Present
	Possible	Possible
Intimacy	Present	Present
	Possible	Possible
Questions me	Present	Present
	Possible	Possible
Confronts me	Present	Present
	Possible	Possible
Simulation	Present	Present
	Possible	Possible

Exercise 15.9

HOW TO BEAT STRESS

Many different effective techniques may be utilized to beat stress. The following are just a few ideas. Review the ones you have learned from this Module. You may want to refer to other techniques, books, and/or materials provided by your trainer.

GOALS

In this exercise you will learn

1. to look at some of the examples of coping with stress, and

2. to think about your long-range goal of work in stress and moving toward a healthier life style.

DIRECTIONS

1. Take time to relax. Develop a form of relaxation that works for you, and don't feel guilty about your new method. Many have used such aids as tapes, yoga, breathing, guided energy. The following may help give you an idea of how to relax.

   Here is how this stress reduction idea works:

   > Picture a calm scene (the hypothalamus is initiating reactions inside of you) that causes you to feel that sense of calmness. If you desire, you can review an actual picture of that scene or "see" the scene by the way of music that rekindles the situation in your mind's eye.

   The thoughts that occupy our minds are the thoughts that guide our actions. Mental relaxation is a key to reducing stress or anxiety. Techniques used have different names but are similar because they involve breathing techniques. The basic technique follows:

   - Sit or lie down.

   - Uncross your arms or legs.

   - Shut your eyes.

   - Breathe in through your nose.

   - Count internally to three as you do that.

   - Breathe out through your mouth to a count of five.

   - Do this cycle of breathing 10 times.

   - Visualize yourself in a positive scene.

- See the scene in great detail.

- See yourself doing only positive things.

- After three to five minutes just drift "awake."

After your short but relaxing experience, reclose your eyes and "see" three positive things you will want to do:

- One for yourself.

- One for a person whom you have not seen or with whom you have not been in touch for a while.

- One for a person you see and interact with every day.

You control reduction of stress by initiating some action that puts you back in a leadership role.

2. Talk out your problems. The stress of holding in your worries and anxieties can eventually make you sick. When problems build up, talk them out with a friend or a professional counselor. Use techniques learned in this book to help you discuss them.

3. Plan your tasks so you can easily handle them. You should plan your work including household chores so you do things one step at a time. Planning allows you to pace yourself. Some of the ideas in Module 16 may be helpful.

4. Deal with anger. Vent your steam. This is far better than holding it inside. You may want to refer to assertiveness training (Module 10) or confrontation (Module 11) to help you express your anger.

5. Get away for a while. Getting yourself involved in something entirely removed from what you do all the time is an excellent way of getting your mind off your problems. Build exercise and leisure into your life. Develop other interests.

6. Be realistic in your goals. Don't get caught in the overachievement syndrome—taking on more than you can accomplish. Most of us have limits and it's important to recognize them. Sooner or later we all have to say, "No, I don't think I should try for that."

7. Avoid self-medication. Make sure you don't fall into the trap of trying to relieve your stress by turning to chemicals. Look at Module 14 to help you look at your own method.

8. Learn to accept what you can't change. You may want to think differently about things you can't change. You may want to change negative into positive thinking.

9. Look after your body. Do you exercise on a regular basis? The whole area of exercise for healthier lifestyles is very important. One needs to exercise at least three times a week in a vigorous manner. It is really neat to get into an activity that is fun and healthful.

10. Look after your diet. As for food, the best thing for you is to eat three times a day with a proper balance of nutrients. Look at your diet and see if you need to get involved in a program for weight reduction or proper diet. Look at your intake of caffeine, sugar, salt, and alcohol. It may be causing you problems.

Exercise 15.10

Name _____

Date _____ Hour _____

LONG-RANGE GOALS

By now you are thinking in terms of weeks and months ahead, are planning on things you want to achieve, and are setting new goals for yourself. In this exercise you are to record some of those long-range goals.

GOALS

In this exercise you will

1. identify your long-range goals, and

2. record your long-range goals for later analysis of achievements.

DIRECTIONS

1. Review *"Examples of Long-range Goals"* for mental, physical, and emotional areas.

2. Write a long-range goal for yourself in each of the three areas on the form entitled *"My Long-range Goals."*

3. Use the *"Long-Range Goal Setting Form"* to help you formulate and analyze your goal(s).

4. Review with another trainee your long-range goals and plans (techniques) for achievement.

5. Submit your goals to the trainer for review.

EXAMPLES OF LONG-RANGE GOALS

1. Mental Area—learn relaxation through imagery. Practice every morning.

2. Physical Area—run one mile daily and learn to play tennis.

3. Emotional Area—make one new friend that I can talk to, get more involved in my church group, and have fun with my mother at least once a week.

Exercise 15.10 (Continued)

MY LONG-RANGE GOALS

1. **Mental Area**

   schedual my time better so that my stress level will not be so high

2. **Physical Area**

   continue to run track and keep in shape even after the season is over

3. **Emotional Area**

   try to think more positively and make more friends and to be open to people

Exercise 15.10 (Continued)　　　　　　Name _____

　　　　　　　　　　　　　　　　　　Date _____ Hour _____

LONG-RANGE GOAL SETTING FORM

1. What is your long-range goal? State one.

　　　　　　to enrole in a good college

2. How soon, realistically would you like to achieve your goal?

　　　　　　within the next year

3. What present strengths do you possess that will help you achieve this goal?

　　　　good student
　　　　　good grades
　　　　　　above level classes

4. What new strengths might be required to achieve this goal?

　　　　better studying habits,
　　　　　more responsible
　　　　　　new variety of people

5. What barriers, if any, do you anticipate that might keep you from achieving your goal?

6. The goal is (check off)　realistic　　　　✓

　　　　　　　　　　　measurable　　　____

　　　　　　　　　　　desirable　　　　____

　　　　　　　　　　　stated positively　____

Exercise 15.10 (Continued)

7. Write your plan for accomplishing your goal.

   Include:

   a. Positive message to yourself.

   b. Daily or weekly activities.

   c. Weekly progress checkpoints. (Includes attainment of your short-term goals.)

   d. Description of your personal support group and what specifically you need from them to help you attain the goal.

   e. Other points that you consider to be important.

MODULE XVI

ENHANCING SELF-ESTEEM

MODULE **16**

ENHANCING
SELF-ESTEEM

The following exercises are to help individuals develop positive feelings about themselves and to view themselves as capable of developing and changing through examination of their own strengths, successes, and values and by teaching individuals how to set goals and act on them.

In examining your present self-esteem, it is important to get in touch with where your self-esteem came from. Often it comes from our friends and families. Each of us needs to accept ourselves in order to keep satisfying relationships with others. Self-esteem means accepting yourself for whom you really are and believing that you are indeed a worthwhile person who is deserving of love and respect from others.

Self-esteem is our sense of how good we feel about ourselves. It is based on our judgment of ourselves, not on other individuals' assessment. Self-esteem is the key to long-term management of stress. A positive self-esteem gives us the ability to handle stressors in our daily lives.

Use. This module should be used with a group of individuals who know each other; it also can be used separately or as advanced training. It is best used with adults and high school students. It has been used successfully with adolescents.

Exercise 16.1

Name _____

Date _____ Hour _____

CHECKLIST FOR SELF-ESTEEM

GOALS

In this exercise you will

1. become aware of how you view yourself in terms of confidence,

2. become aware of ways to enhance your self-esteem, and

3. develop a plan of action.

INTRODUCTION

We are often our worst enemies in terms of our feelings about ourselves. The "Self-esteem Checklist" on the following page contains a list of questions that you may want to ask yourself in terms of self-esteem.

DIRECTIONS

1. Answer the questions on the *"Self-esteem Checklist."*

2. Discuss how you see yourself and your self-confidence.

3. Read possible *"Ways of Improving Self-esteem."*

4. Develop a *"Plan for Improving My Self-esteem."*

5. Be aware of how you look and react to individuals in the next few days; do you have high self-esteem or do you need improvement?

Exercise 16.1 (Continued)

SELF-ESTEEM CHECKLIST

	Yes	No	Some-times
1. Do you make your role far more important than it actually is?	—	—	—
2. Are you jealous of the achievements and positions of others?	—	—	—
3. Do you find yourself judging yourself based on standards set by others?	—	—	—
4. Can you share your friends with other friends, or do you have to be the only friend?	—	—	—
5. Is it difficult to admit a mistake or take criticism?	—	—	—
6. Do you put others down so that you can feel okay?	—	—	—
7. Are you a perfectionist?	—	—	—
8. Must you always be a winner in a game?	—	—	—
9. Can you accept compliments?	—	—	—
10. Do you stay away from new things because of fear of failure?	—	—	—
11. Do you neglect your needs because you meet others' needs?	—	—	—
12. Do you have difficulty speaking up for things you want?	—	—	—
13. Do you have difficulty looking at people?	—	—	—

Exercise 16.1 (Continued)

Name _____

Date _____ Hour _____

Based on your responses to the "Self-Esteem Checklist," how would you rate your self-esteem?

____ Excellent

____ Good

____ Needs improvement

WAYS OF IMPROVING SELF-ESTEEM

1. Speak up for yourself.

2. Don't put yourself down.

3. Take charge of your life.

4. Don't feel sorry for yourself.

5. Do things for yourself.

6. Be proud of yourself.

7. Take care of your needs first.

Exercise 16.1 (Continued)

PLAN FOR IMPROVING MY SELF-ESTEEM

Exercise 16.2

Name _____

Date _____ Hour _____

MESSAGES FROM THE PAST

GOALS

In this exercise you will

1. become aware of the messages from your past that influence you, and

2. discuss ways to change these messages.

INTRODUCTION

The thoughts that we have about ourselves often come from our past. These messages contribute to our level of self-esteem. These messages can be positive or negative.

DIRECTIONS

1. On the following sheet, *"People and Their Messages from the Past,"* write the messages that you recall receiving from individuals who have been important to you.

2. Be aware of messages from the past that influence the present and develop ways to change THE NEGATIVE ONES!

Exercise 16.2 (Continued)

PEOPLE AND THEIR MESSAGES FROM THE PAST

Examples: **Mother:** "You can always do better."
Father: "I know you can do it."
Teacher: "You surely do try hard."
Brother: "You're fat!"

Mother:

Father:

Grandparents:

Siblings:

Friends:

Teachers:

Boss:

Coach:

Others:(Identify)

_____:

_____:

_____:

_____:

Which of these messages still affect your self-esteem?

Can you change some of these messages?

Exercise 16.3

Name _____

Date _____ Hour _____

STRENGTHS

Too frequently we are unable to focus on our strengths. This exercise will assist you in looking at your strengths.

GOALS

In this exercise you will

1. become aware of your individual strengths,

2. identify significant good events in your life, and

3. learn to feel positively about yourself and other group members.

DIRECTIONS

1. Work with the leader in the introduction and unfoldment.

2. Share, when the trainer asks you to do so, significant events of your life—good moments, good events, good relationships, successes, rewards, and so forth.

3. Sit in a circle. Write your name at the top of the other side of this sheet of paper.

4. Notice the example given where other participants recorded positive personal characteristics in Column A and skills in Column B regarding another trainee named Pat.

5. On the part of each participant, pass the paper to the left. Each person in the group is to write one positive personality characteristic and one skill developed by the person whose name is on the paper. Each person's paper is passed to every group member so that each group member receives positive feedback from every other member.

6. After all the papers are completed, have the list of positive personality characteristics and developed skills read by each participant to the entire group. At this time the group members describe in behavioral terms the criteria by which they measure the development of the skill.

Exercise 16.3 (Continued)

EXAMPLE

Name _____Pat_____

Column A Positive Personal Characteristics	Column B Skills
Friendliness	Creativity
Openness	Ability to use fantasy play
Genuineness	Firmness

If the group feels that Pat is creative in the group, they would give an example during the group discussion of when and how she has used her creativity within the group.

Column A Positive Personal Characeristics	Column B Skills

Exercise 16.4

Name _____

Date _____ Hour _____

PERSONAL COAT OF ARMS

GOAL

In this exercise you will learn more about some of the values you hold very dear to you and to publicly state them.

DIRECTIONS

1. In the figure entitled *"Personal Coat of Arms"* draw two pictures in Block 1. One picture is to show something at which you are very good and one is to show something at which you want to become good.

2. Draw a picture in Block 2 to show one of the values from which you would never budge. This is one about which you feel extremely strong, and which you would never give up.

3. Draw a picture in Block 3 to show a value by which your family lives. Make it one that everyone in your family would probably agree is one of their most important.

4. Imagine that you could achieve anything you wanted and that whatever you tried to do would be a success. What would you strive to do? Symbolize this by a drawing in Block 4.

5. Use Block 5 to symbolize one of the values in which you wished all people would believe and certainly one in which you believe very deeply.

6. Write four words in Block 6 that you would like people to say about you behind your back.

7. Discuss your Coat of Arms with participants in your training group.

PERSONAL COAT OF ARMS

1.	2.
3.	4.
5.	6.

NOTE: Our thanks to Sr. Louise, Principal of St. Julian's School in Chicago.

Exercise 16.5

VALUES AUCTION

GOAL

In this exercise you will learn how to set priorities for important things in your life.

GENERAL DIRECTIONS FOR THE AUCTION

1. Instruct each group member that he/she has the sum of $20,000 of make believe money to use to purchase the various items to be auctioned. Ask participants to examine the items on the *"Auction"* form and to "budget" the $20,000 among the various items.

2. Hold the auction with one member serving as auctioneer.

3. During the auction the participants keep track of the items on which they have bid or won by noting the highest amount bid for each item and whether or not they won it.

4. After the auction, rank individually the items in order of the amount bid on them. For example, if your highest bid on an item was $800 for a roomful of pennies, then this could be first on your list. Using the following key have each participant assess which values played an active part in his/her bidding.

Key

1 + 18	justice	10 + 27	power
2 + 19	altruism	11 + 28	love
3 + 20	recognition	12 + 29	aesthetic talent
4 + 21	achievement	13 + 30	physical achievements
5 + 22	pleasure	14 + 31	physical well-being
6 + 23	wisdom	15 + 32	emotional well-being
7 + 24	honesty	16 + 33	knowledge
8 + 25	autonomy	17 + 34	religion
9 + 26	economic security		

DIRECTIONS FOR YOU

1. Participate in the auction.

2. Assess your values.

3. Discuss the experience among trainees and what was gained.

AUCTION

Items to Be Auctioned	Amount You Budgeted	Highest Amount You Bid	Items Won
1. To rid the world of prejudice.			
2. To serve the sick and needy.			
3. To become a famous figure (movie star, baseball hero, astronaut, etc.)			
4. A project that will triple your family's income this year.			
5. A year of daily massage and the world's finest cuisine from the world's best chef.			
6. To know the meaning of life.			
7. A vaccine to make all persons incapable of lying.			
8. The opportunity to set your own working conditions.			
9. To be the richest person in the world.			
10. The Presidency of the United States.			
11. To love and be loved by someone very special to you.			
12. A house overlooking the most beautiful view in the world, in which you may keep for a year 40 of your favorite works of art.			

Exercise 16.5 (Continued)

Name _____

Date _____ Hour _____

Items to Be Auctioned	Amount You Budgeted	Highest Amount You Bid	Items Won
13. To be considered the most attractive person in the state.			
14. To live to 100 with no illness.			
15. To know all about yourself and know for sure who you are.			
16. A complete center of learning with all the learning aids available.			
17. An audience with the spiritual leader either past or present that you most admire.			
18. To rid the world of unfairness.			
19. To donate $1 million to your favorite charity.			
20. To be voted "Outstanding Person of the Year" and praised in every newspaper in the world.			
21. To master the profession of your choice.			
22. A year with nothing to do but enjoy yourself, with all needs and desires automatically met.			
23. For one year to be the wisest person in the world, and to make only right decisions.			

Exercise 16.5 (Continued)

Items to Be Auctioned	Amount You Budgeted	Highest Amount You Bid	Items Won
24. To sneak authenticity serum into every water supply in the world.			
25. To do your own thing without hassling.			
26. A roomful of pennies.			
27. To control the destinies of 500,000 people.			
28. To live in a world where all people give and receive love.			
29. Unlimited travel and tickets to attend any concert, opera, or ballet for a year.			
30. A total make-over: a new hair style, all new wardrobe from the designer of your choice, two weeks at a beauty spa such as Main Chance.			
31. Membership in a great health club.			
32. Antihangup pill.			
33. Your own ominiscent computer for any facts you might need.			
34. To spend six months with the greatest religious figure of your faith, past or present.			

Permission Granted: Achievement Motivation Program, Chicago, IL.

Exercise 16.6

STRENGTH ACKNOWLEDGEMENT

GOAL

In this exercise you will learn to encourage persons to affirm their own personal strengths and assets and to receive positive feedback from other persons.

DIRECTIONS

1. Ask for volunteers after the process has been explained.

2. As a volunteer, list "Self-perceived Strengths" in the space provided. Record those strengths that you are willing to acknowledge and the conditions/situations under which you see yourself most likely to show those strengths.

3. As a volunteer, invite group members for affirmation by asking, "What strengths do you see in me?"

4. As a volunteer, ask, if you so desire, "What is keeping me from using my strengths?" This is not intended as a focus on weakness or a negative criticism. The intent is clearly in the statement, "What is keeping me from using my strengths?"

SELF-PERCEIVED STRENGTHS

Strengths I will acknowledge	Conditions/Situations where I am most likely to show these strengths

Exercise 16.7

Name _____

Date _____ Hour _____

JOURNEY INTO LIFE: GOAL SETTING

In this phase, we begin to take ourselves out of this group and into the real world. We're going to set some goals for ourselves; short- and long-term.

GOALS

In this exercise you will

1. identify and write short-term goals for your own life,

2. share and obtain feedback from fellow trainees on your own goals, and

3. identify and write one long-term goal and will share it with your alter-ego (a fellow trainee) who will give you feedback at a later date.

DIRECTIONS FOR SHORT-TERM GOALS

1. Write one or two short-term goals that you can and will accomplish before we meet as a group again.

2. Tackle a *real* problem or job—an authentic, worthy one.

3. Make your goal be realistic, achievable within time and space limits.

4. Select goals that you want to do, not because someone else wants you to, although it may involve significant others.

5. State your goal in action words not being or attitudinal words. "I will do (something)."

6. Write your goals so that each is measurable. Exactly how much will you do? How much progress and not just, "I'll study math for twenty hours."

7. Evaluate action necessary to achieve your goals and make sure that your action will not be harmful to yourself or another.

8. Share your goals with other trainees and help each other to analyze goals written to assure that each meet criteria listed in directions 1 through 7.

My Short-term Goals

1.

2.

Exercise 16.7 (Continued)

DIRECTIONS FOR LONG-TERM GOALS

1. With your alter-ego (another trainee who has agreed to serve in the role of your alter-ego), set an achievement goal for one year (9 to 15 months).

2. Talk about your long-term goal with other trainee and discuss it in depth with your alter-ego.

3. Set only one long-term goal.

4. Make sure your goal is something you would not have done as a matter of course. If possible, it should be new and challenging. It may be something important you've been hoping to do but thinking you probably couldn't or wouldn't.

5. Write your alter-ego's address and phone number. Promise to report your goal achievement to him/her within the time limits you set. (Do it.)

My Long-term Goal

Record your goal here and give a copy of it to your alter-ego.

My Alter-ego

Name

Street Address

City, State, ZIP

Telephone Number

David Leverage

- good listener / always there
you always know when I need a
hug or just a big smile
- you're a funny and compasionate
guy - I know you can always
cheer me up! :)
- you're really funny and
such a church-boy (NOT!)
I'm glad we've gotten to
be better friends.
- I've known you for a long time. And
you are one of the most caring guys I
know. You are an awesome friend
- Just talking w/you gives me a
feeling of relief as in things
aren't so bad & I see the other side
& when you make me laugh I can't
quit
- You are so funny David. I have so
much to say, but I don't think that
it could fit all on here. You are a very
compassionate young man and you make
me feel "wanted". I don't think the word
wanted was the right word but oh well, you get the point

- I'm glad we're in the same group b/c I have another guy to talk to. You are really fun to be with and you have a great personality.

Exercise 16.8

Name _____

Date _____ Hour _____

CONCLUSION

GOAL

In this exercise you will learn to gain feedback from others in the group.

DIRECTIONS

1. Write your name on the top of the back side of this page. (See alternate procedure as listed on next page.)

2. Pass your sheet to your left so that another participant can write a word or phrase that describes a strength or good quality about you.

3. Write on the paper that is passed to you.

4. Continue to pass the paper until everyone has written on each card.

5. Pass these papers around again, and each participant writes an "I urge you to . . ." telegram.

6. As a group, discuss the comments written so that participants can explain what they wrote.

Exercise 16.8 (Continued)

This sheet is for the person to keep whose name appears above. Other trainees will share information to assist the person named.

WORDS OR PHRASE to describe a strength, attribute, good quality, possessed by the person named above.

POSITIVE SUGGESTIONS to help the person named above to achieve even more in the future. Send a telegram with the words "I urge you to . . ."

Alternate Procedure: Distribute as many cards with your name on each as there are trainees. Ask them to write a positive statement about you on one side of the card and on the other side to write "I urge you . . ." suggestion to help you focus on a change that would assist you.

MODULE XVII

LEADERSHIP TRAINING

MODULE **17**

LEADERSHIP TRAINING

Many opportunities exist for providing leadership to a group. Group leaders do not necessarily automatically know how to be good leaders; usually they must go through training. The training that you have learned in earlier modules will help you to be a better listener and questioner, but often when we are put in a leadership role we are not able to accomplish what is needed. The reasons are many: sometimes the group will not cooperate, sometimes we put things off and we cannot accomplish our plans, and sometimes we are not sure of our role as leader.

Leadership can be a fun and rewarding activity in which to participate, but it also can be frustrating and unrewarding. The purpose of this module is to assist individuals in learning how to be effective leaders so that placed in a leadership role they will gain the most from that position and accomplish what is expected.

Use. This module can be used for training of elected officers and committee chairpersons or it can be used as basic training for group discussion. This module can be used for high school or older adults and can be used separately or following the other modules. If it is used separately, then a good procedure might be to teach attending, empathy, and questioning skills in Modules 4, 6, and 8 (*Book 1, Introductory Program*). These skills could be used to assist with organizational training or support group leadership training.

Exercise 17.1

Name _____

Date _____ Hour _____

LEADERSHIP STYLE PROFILE

Often we have difficulty when asked to lead a certain kind of group. Some of us like to jump in and get things done and others like to discuss and get others to cooperate. To be an effective leader you need to know your style of leadership—whether you are more effective as a task leader (T) or as a people leader (P).

GOAL

In this exercise you will learn to evaluate yourself in terms of task orientation and people orientation.

DIRECTIONS

1. Fill out the *"T-P Leadership Questionnaire."*

2. Listen to your trainer discuss the different types of leadership.

3. Score your questionnaire.

4. Discuss your results with the group.

T-P LEADERSHIP QUESTIONNAIRE

The following items describe aspects of leadership behavior. Respond to each item according to the way you would be most likely to act if you were the leader of a work group. Circle if you would be likely to behave in the described way: Always (A), Frequently (F), Occasionally (O), Seldom (S), or Never (N).

"If I were the leader of a work group . . ."

A   F   O   S   N   _____   1. I would most likely act as the spokesman of the group.

A   F   O   S   N   _____   2. I would encourage overtime work.

A   F   O   S   N   _____   3. I would allow members complete freedom in their work.

A   F   O   S   N   _____   4. I would encourage the use of uniform procedures.

A   F   O   S   N   _____   5. I would permit the members to use their own judgment in solving problems.

A   F   O   S   N   _____   6. I would like to be in charge of competing groups.

A   F   O   S   N   _____   7. I would speak as a representative of the group.

A   F   O   S   N   _____   8. I would needle members for greater effort.

A   F   O   S   N   _____   9. I would try out my ideas on the group.

A   F   O   S   N   _____   10. I would let the members do their work the way they feel best.

A   F   O   S   N   _____   11. I would be working hard for a promotion.

A   F   O   S   N   _____   12. I would be able to tolerate postponement and uncertainty.

A   F   O   S   N   _____   13. I would speak for the group when visitors are present

A   F   O   S   N   _____   14. I would keep the work moving at a rapid pace.

A   F   O   S   N   _____   15. I would turn the members loose on a job and let them go to it.

A   F   O   S   N   _____   16. I would settle conflicts when they occur in the room.

Exercise 17.1 (Continued)

A   F   O   S   N   _____   17. I would get swamped by details.

A   F   O   S   N   _____   18. I would represent the group at outside meetings.

A   F   O   S   N   _____   19. I would be reluctant to allow the members any freedom of action.

A   F   O   S   N   _____   20. I would decide what shall be done and how it shall be done.

A   F   O   S   N   _____   21. I would push for increased production.

A   F   O   S   N   _____   22. I would let some members have authority that they could keep.

A   F   O   S   N   _____   23. I predict that things would usually work out.

A   F   O   S   N   _____   24. I would allow the group a high degree of initiative.

A   F   O   S   N   _____   25. I would assign group members to particular tasks.

A   F   O   S   N   _____   26. I would ask the members to work harder.

A   F   O   S   N   _____   27. I would trust the group members to exercise good judgment.

A   F   O   S   N   _____   28. I would schedule the work to be done.

A   F   O   S   N   _____   29. I would refuse to explain my actions.

A   F   O   S   N   _____   30. I would persuade the others that my ideas are to their advantage.

A   F   O   S   N   _____   31. I would permit the group to set its own pace.

A   F   O   S   N   _____   32. I would urge the group to better its previous record.

A   F   O   S   N   _____   33. I would act without consulting the group.

A   F   O   S   N   _____   34. I would ask the group members to follow standard rules and regulations.

A   F   O   S   N   _____   35. I would ask that group members follow standard rules and regulations

TOTAL SCORES   T _____   P _____ (To find score read the next section)

NOTE: The "*T-P Leadership Questionnaire*" is from T.J. Sergiovanni, R. Metzcus, and L. Burden, "Toward a particularistic approach to leadership style: Some findings," *American Educational Research Journal*, 1969, 6. 62-79.

Reprinted from: *A Handbook of Structured Experiences for Human Relations Training, Volume I*, J. William Pfeiffer and John E. Jones, Editors. San Diego, CA: Copyright 1984. Used with permission.

LEADERSHIP STYLE PROFILE

The *"T-P Leadership Questionnaire"* is used to evaluate your dimensions of task orientation (T) and people orientation (P).

1. Circle the item number for questionnaire items 8, 12, 17, 18, 19, 30, 34, and 35.

2. Write a "1" in front of the circled items to which you responded "S" (Seldom) or "N" (Never).

3. Write a "1" in front of the items not circled to which you responded "A" (Always) or "F" (Frequently).

4. Count the circled "1's." This is your score for concern for people. Record the score in the blank following the letter "P" at the end of the questionnaire.

5. Count the uncircled "1's." This is your score for concern for tasks. Record this number in the blank following the letter "T."

Exercise 17.1 (Continued)

Name _____

Date _____ Hour _____

EVALUATING DIRECTIONS

To indicate your style of leadership, first find the number that represents your score on the concern for task dimension (T) on the left-hand arrow. Next, move to the right-hand arrow and find the number that represents your score on the concern for people dimension (P).

Draw a straight line that connects the P and T score; the point at which that line crosses the team "Shared Leadership" arrow indicates your score on that dimension.

Exercise 17.1 (Continued)

AUTOCRATIC LEADERSHIP	SHARED LEADERSHIP	LASSEZ-FAIRE LEADERSHIP
High Productivity	High Morale and High Productivity	High Morale

```
     .                      .                          .

15 ·                        .                        · 15
     .                      .                        .
       .                    .                      .
         .                  .                    .
           .                .                  .
10    ·                     .                · 10
        .                   .              .
          .                 .            .
            .               .          .
              .             .        .
 5 ·                        .       · 5
     .                      .     .
       .                    .   .
         .                  . .
T—Concern                          P—Concern
for Task        .     .     .      for People


                            .

                            0
```

Shared Leadership Resulting from Relating
Concern for Task and Concern for People

Exercise 17.2

Name _____

Date _____ Hour _____

LEADING A DISCUSSION GROUP

Many leaders are called on to lead a discussion group concerning an important topic. Often this skill is just putting together some of the skills learned earlier and used with a group of people.

GOALS

In this exercise you will learn

1. to understand some basic concepts of discussion group leadership, and

2. to practice leading a discussion group.

DIRECTIONS

1. Read the information concerning skills of the discussion leader.

2. Discuss the information.

3. Form groups of five, one person playing the leader; one person, the observer.

4. Take one of the sample leadership topics and discuss it for 15 minutes. Get feedback from the observer.

5. As observer, use the *Observer Evaluation Form.*

6. Repeat the process until everyone has been both a discussion leader and an observer.

SKILLS OF THE DISCUSSION LEADER

The two building blocks of a good group session are acceptance and listening. When the discussion leader is going to meet with the group, it is important for the leader to get the group into a circle as quickly as possible. The participants can sit on the floor or in chairs, but they must be in a circle. Why a circle? Everybody has equal status; all members of a circle can see and communicate with all other members.

The leader must understand that in any circle discussion two things should be happening: acceptance and listening.

1. Acceptance

    a. The process of accepting is the process of taking or receiving freely, without stops or hesitation, any and every communication offered. In particular, the leader accepts from the participants; participants also accept from each other and may possibly accept from the leader.

    b. In the process of accepting various interactions should be taking place. The discussion leader needs to take communications or contributions made, taking them as completely as possible and with unconditional acceptance. This means developing the ability to accept honestly as worthwhile and valid every contribution any member of the group makes. You must attempt to get across to participants by this acceptance of their communications and contributions that they themselves are okay. You are expressing to them that you like them as people and accept them just as they are. In group procedure, when a discussion leader has been able to develop this attitude of acceptance, the group members will participate more freely and will be more able and willing to discuss their genuine concerns.

2. Listening

    As the discussion leader, you will serve as the model. You will set the stage by listening carefully to participants. Use both nonverbal and verbal methods to indicate to participants that you are listening. Some examples of nonverbal behavior are the way you sit, your facial expression, and your hand motions. Your verbal methods can be restating their questions, reflecting on what they have said, or encouragement of the quiet participants. These verbal and nonverbal acknowledgement methods will indicate to participants that you are listening. They will model after you and they also will begin to listen. Use techniques learned earlier in training.

SOME QUESTIONING TECHNIQUES IN THE CIRCLE

Questioning is a vital role to play in the group. Remember, however, that questioning can be either helpful or harmful to the group process. A good rule to follow is to avoid questions that make participants feel defensive or feel that they have to justify their actions. In most cases, questions that ask "why" threaten participants. Open-ended questions encourage participants to go into the experience of discussions more easily. Some examples of open-ended questions are as follows:

"Would you like to tell us more about that?"

"What was it like for you when such and such was happening?"

"How did you feel when that happened?"

"Is there more that you would like to say?"

"Tells us what other feelings you had."

When asking what, where, and how questions, don't give participants the feeling that they are being grilled. Another questioning and listening technique is just to respond to the participant's statement with something like:

"You really sounded excited when you told us about that."

"It sounds as though you never really got over that experience."

Really you are opening the door to participants and, though you are not saying so exactly, you are expressing the thought that if they want to talk more about it, the group will listen.

QUESTIONS THAT CLARIFY

Ask questions that help participants clarify in their own minds what the experience was or what the feeling was. Some examples of this type of question are as follows:

"What did you do when it happened?"

"Do you think many people feel that way?"

"Do any of you have any questions you would like to ask Mrs. Ruque?"

BASIC WAYS TO KEEP THE DISCUSSION GOING

Raise pivotal questions.

Turn questions back to the group.

Allow silences for reflections.

Show acceptance by nodding, using positive words or key words.

Have participants to respond to each other rather than to the discussion leader.

SAMPLE TOPICS

1. The participant council has $500 to spend in the next month. We need to decide by this meeting how it would be spent.

2. Discuss your feelings about the military draft.

3. Discuss ways to be supportive of someone trying to lose weight.

4. Discuss whether or not the proposed XYZ Committee should be allowed to form.

5. Assume the group is a family and discuss whether or not the offer to purchase the family home should be accepted.

6. Assume you are the Publicity Committee within a local service club and are meeting to decide committee projects for the year.

Exercise 17.2 (Continued)

OBSERVER EVALUATION FORM

Skills

Place a check mark under "High," "Medium," or "Low," designating how you rate the discussion leader's skill level for each group-leading skill listed.

	High	Medium	Low
Accepting	_____	_____	_____
Listening	_____	_____	_____
Questioning	_____	_____	_____

In the same manner, rate the group members' response levels:

	High	Medium	Low
Trusting	_____	_____	_____
Resistant or reluctant	_____	_____	_____
Defensive	_____	_____	_____
Responsive to other group members	_____	_____	_____
Expressive of feelings	_____	_____	_____
Expressive of thoughts (variety and depth)	_____	_____	_____

Comments: _____

_____

_____

Exercise 17.3

Name _____

Date _____ Hour _____

WORKING WITH OTHERS

GOALS

In this exercise you will learn

1. how you relate to others,

2. that individuals who are different have different strengths than you do, and

3. how you motivate others.

INTRODUCTION

As a leader, you need to be able to work with others. Often individuals who are very different from you are difficult for you to work with because you feel threatened or challenged. If you can see the strengths in others and utilize them to get the job done, they you will be a more effective leader. If you also understand that individuals need recognition for their efforts, you also will be a better leader. To begin you need to understand how you relate to others.

DIRECTIONS

1. Think of the times that you have been working on a project, not as leader but a participant, and the group members were not getting along because they were different.

2. Identify the strengths of the group.

3. Identify strengths of the group members that possibly could have been used to help the group.

4. Think of ways that members of your group could have been motivated to assist.

5. Role play your own situation or use the following role play example.

    You are the leader of a group that is committed to getting Sam elected. You as a leader are good at generally knowing what needs to be done, but you are not good with finances or detail work. You also are not good at talking with individuals who are of a different culture. You have an opportunity to develop a team that will get Sam elected:

    • What types of individuals do you need on your team?

    • How will you work with them?

    • What might be some problems?

    • How can you overcome these problems?

    Role play a group planning meeting with the group members playing characters that you think up. Focus on motivating individuals through recognition and listening to their ideas.

OBSERVATION REPORT

6. Following the role playing, review your observations of the leader.

   How well did the leader

   a. Utilize the members that are different?

   b. Motivated the group members through

       Encouragement, Listening, and Questioning?

7. Think of a group that you presently lead:

   • How do you relate to the different members?

   • How do you utilize their differences?

   • How do you motivate the members of your group?

Exercise 17.4

Name _____

Date _____ Hour _____

TIME MANAGEMENT

GOALS

In this exercise you will

1. look at your own obstacles to effective time management,

2. look at how you presently handle time, and

3. develop ways to manage time differently so that you get the maximum benefit from your time.

INTRODUCTION

Time management is sometimes one of the biggest stumbling blocks to effective leadership. Individuals generally handle time differently. Some individuals like to plan things in advance, while others like to do things at the last minute. The bottom line is, do they get the task done? To work effectively you need to understand your own approach to managing time. Also recognize that some obstacles exist to effective time management. Individuals can be trained in managing their time.

DIRECTIONS

1. Look at the list of *"Obstacles to Effective Time Management."*

2. List some long-term and some short-term goals that you may have.

3. Keep a chart of how you used your time yesterday by completing the chart entitled *"My Day."*

4. Decide what are your time wasters.

5. Complete the two items under *"Goals."*

6. Develop an action plan to use time differently.

7. Keep a chart of how you spend your time.

8. Keep a journal of how to change time.

9. Learn to prioritize activities each day.

10. Balance your activities ("have to," "want to").

OBSTACLES TO EFFECTIVE TIME MANAGEMENT

Procrastination

This is putting off an event or an activity. The greater the value of the event the greater is the distress that results from putting it off. It may be overwhelming, distasteful.

Corrections:

- Live in the now, not the future. Use every minute.
- Get started on something that you have been putting off.
- Decide not to be tired.
- Get rid of critical messages from the past.
- Reduce worry.
- Take action.
- Be creative.

Perfectionism

Perfectionists tend to spend an overabundance of time and energy on few tasks at the expense of others, and this can cause a lot of stress. Perfectionists are likely to have difficulty maintaining a satisfactory balance in the time they devote to the self, family, and job. There is much stress in the life of a perfectionist.

Possible correction:

- Look at the hitting average of most professional batters: 300 is very good (hitting a ball 3 out of 10 times).
- After setting goals, set out to accomplish them.
- View unfinished work as an opportunity.
- What is worth doing is "worth doing," not worth doing perfectly.

Fear of Failure

If you fear failure, then your self-image is threatened, and this can lead to stress.

Corrections:

- Practice positive images.
- Separate actions from self-confidence.
- Do activities that are related to your fear.

Do you use any of these time wasters? _____ Yes _____ No

How can you correct these?

Exercise 17.4 (Continued)

Name _____

Date _____ Hour _____

GOALS

My long-range goals are

My short-range goals are

MY DAY

1. In the first column of space provided make a list of all the activities you did yesterday.

2. In the second column note how much time you spent on each one.

3. In the third and fourth columns identify your priorities for that day (1,2,3): Want to do/Have to Do.

4. In the fifth and sixth columns check those activities that fit into your long-term (LT) and/or short-term (ST) goals.

Activities	Amount of Time	Priorities		My Goals	
		Want to	Have to	LT	ST

5. How can I change my time to fit my long-term and short-term goals?

6. How can I eliminate time wasters?

Exercise 17.5

DEVELOPING AN ACTION PLAN

As leaders, we often do not have a plan of action for the task we are to accomplish. A wise procedure is to set aside ahead of time your specific objectives that you are planning and have the time line organized.

GOALS

In this exercise you will learn

1. to understand the components of a plan of action, and

2. to write an action plan for a leadership role.

DIRECTIONS

1. Read the *"Action Plan Components."*

2. Read the *"Sample Program Plan of Action."*

3. Divide into clusters of two.

4. Working with your trainee partner, develop your own action plan for your leadership position by completing the *"Program Plan of Action Form."* If you do not have a trainee partner, assume one that would be in keeping with one you hope to have.

5. Complete the *"Commitment to Action Form."*

ACTION PLAN COMPONENTS

1. Statement of Need

   Briefly describe the nature of the need in the program area. State how the need was determined (i.e., survey, Executive Committee, National Office, other).

2. Goals

   State the major goals (expectations) that the program will strive to accomplish to meet identified needs. Needs can be translated quite easily into goal statements. Goals will be general and broad in nature. List goals in order of their priority. Indicate those goals that you believe will be accomplished over a longer period of time (two to five years).

3. Objectives

   For each stated goal of the program, specific measurable objectives should be stated for accomplishing the goal. Objectives should be stated in terms of desired changes, activities, and so on; which if accomplished, will result in goal attainment. Objectives, well stated, provide the necessary directions for procedures, evaluation, and allocation of funds.

4. Procedures

    The procedure will essentially respond to these three questions:

    a. How will the objectives be implemented?

    b. Who will have the responsibility to implement the objectives?

    c. By what time schedule will the procedures for objectives be carried out?

    For each objective relate what are deemed to be the most appropriate procedures or activities to be implemented to accomplish the objective. Several procedures may be suggested for each objective. Procedures may include use of other resources (e.g., people, materials).

    Identify one or more persons with specific and/or collective responsibilities for any one procedure or activity. Relating role and responsibility of a leader appropriate to a particular task is extremely important.

    In determining procedures to be followed, try to establish a time line or time schedule for implementation and completion of activities. Place each procedure into written form. Dates should be as realistic as possible because they can be a useful device for maintaining progress toward goal attainment and for assisting with evaluation.

5. Authority

    The plan must be consistent with the regulations (i.e., By-laws, Constitution) of the organization. In addition, approval by committee, executive board, and/or membership is vital.

6. Cost

    The investment of time, personnel, effort, and money must be carefully considered. Specifically, the expenditures of funds may determine the priority assigned to a given goal or objective and the effect each will have on the total budget. In some instances the process may need to be modified to bring it in line with realistic budget expenditures.

7. Evaluation

    Monitoring and evaluation of all program efforts should be an ongoing effort. The evaluation may be based on the degree of accomplishment of those components of the overall plan of the program. Is the program doing what was stated in objectives and procedures and to what extent? Analysis of evaluation information provides the feedback necessary to determine the effectiveness of program efforts.

Exercise 17.5 (Continued)

Name _____

Date _____ Hour _____

SAMPLE PROGRAM PLAN OF ACTION

PROGRAM GOALS

1. Organize and call Board Meetings

2.

3.

PROGRAM TITLE

Club Organization

PERSON RESPONSIBLE

Tom Smith, President

PROGRAM PLAN DATE

July, 1984

Objective	Procedure	Respon-sibility	Begin Date	End Date	Cost	Status/Evaluation
Set 3 dates this year	Conference, schedule on club calendar	President Officers	July Sept.	Sept. Sept		Scheduled
Set agenda, mail to mem-bership	Ask group; mail	Board Secretary	Oct. Nov.	Oct. Nov.	$20	Scheduled
Establish a regular meet-ing hall for next year.	Mail poll; analyze; rent hall	Secretary Board President	Nov. Nov. Dec.	Nov. Dec. Dec.	$20 $50	Letter done

Exercise 17.5 (Continued)

PROGRAM PLAN OF ACTION

PROGRAM GOALS   PROGRAM TITLE

1.

                                 PERSON RESPONSIBLE

2.

                                 PROGRAM PLAN DATE

3.

Objective	Procedure	Respon-sibility	Begin Date	End Date	Cost	Status/ Evaluation

Exercise 17.5 (Continued)   Name _____

Date _____ Hour _____

COMMITMENT TO ACTION FORM

Name _____   Date _____

I commit and obligate myself to accomplish the following action plan:

1. I plan to _____

   _____

   _____

   _____

   _____

   _____

   _____

   _____

   _____

   _____

2. I have decided on this plan because _____

   _____

   _____

   _____

   _____

   _____

   _____

   _____

   _____

   _____

3. I will accomplish my objectives in the following manner _____

   _____

   _____

   _____

   _____

   _____

   _____

   _____

   _____

Exercise 17.5 (Continued)

4. The person(s) to be involved in my planning and implementation are _____

_____

_____

_____

_____

_____

_____

_____

5. I will complete my objectives by _____

                                                     Month   Day   Year

6. I will evaluate and if necessary revise my commitment:

           _____ Yearly   _____ Monthly   _____ Weekly

                                    (Check one)

Exercise 17.6

Name _____

Date _____ Hour _____

PLANNING PUBLIC RELATIONS

As a leader, you will need to decide which group or groups to contact to assist you in financing and working on your activities. Also you will need to supply different kinds of information to different individuals and groups. For example, obtaining approval for a plan requires different information than is supplied to the news media regarding an activity within the total program.

GOALS

In this exercise you will learn to identify

1. individuals with whom to make contacts inside and outside of the organization, and

2. different kinds of information to be supplied to different individuals and groups.

DIRECTIONS

1. List on the *"Internal and External Contacts"* Form those groups or individuals with whom you may want to communicate in order to increase their understanding of your activities. Use the plan developed in Exercise 17.5.

2. Identify the kinds of information that will be needed for each group and individuals listed in Direction 1.

3. Divide into clusters of two and help each other to review and improve the proposed public relations plans.

INTERNAL AND EXTERNAL CONTACTS

List groups or individuals with whom you may wish to communicate so that they may increase their understanding of your activities. Then identify the kind of information (e.g., request for approval, news release, details of program, financial assistance) that will be supplied to those groups or individuals.

The following example is provided to illustrate how this form might be completed.

Exercise 17.6 (Continued)

For Work Settings

Internal

1. Supervisor
2. Fellow workers
3. Labor union representative

External

1. City officials
2. Residents of geographical area
3. News media

Kind of Information

Request approval of progress
Request cooperation
Request union endorsement and cooperation.

Obtain permit
Request cooperation
News stories of progress

For Organization

Internal

1. Officers
2. Members
3. Board

External

1. State officials
2. Parents
3. Local news media

Kind of Information

Request approval of progress
Copy of approval progress
Request financial assistance

Copy of approval progress with explanation
Information of how children can be involved
News stories of progress

INTERNAL	KIND OF INFORMATION
1. _____	1. _____
2. _____	2. _____
3. _____	3. _____
4. _____	4. _____
5. _____	5. _____
6. _____	6. _____

EXTERNAL	KIND OF INFORMATON
1. _____	1. _____
2. _____	2. _____
3. _____	3. _____
4. _____	4. _____
5. _____	5. _____
6. _____	6. _____

Name _____

Date _____ Hour _____

PLANNING A CONFERENCE OR OTHER MEETINGS

Often we are called to plan a meeting or set up a conference. This job is frequently difficult and nearly always a lot of work. Plan your meeting or conference in three major steps:

1. Consider and record the person-oriented and task-oriented factors contributing to the meeting or conference. Outline related activities that will be performed to account for these factors.

2. Establish conference or meeting particulars such as title, format, place and time, speakers or presentors, and so forth.

3. Coordinate your organizational and operational assistance—list those individuals who will help, the external and internal contacts, sources of materials, and so forth.

GOAL

In this exercise you will learn to plan a meeting or conference.

DIRECTIONS

1. Look at the *"Example Conference"* of a suggested meeting.

2. Work in clusters of three to plan this conference.

3. Complete the *"Conference and Meeting Planning Form."*

4. Share with the entire group your plan when complete.

EXAMPLE CONFERENCE

You have been asked to set up a conference on drug abuse for your church. You have been given complete freedom in terms of how to set it up. You have a budget of $500.00. Use the Conference and Meeting planning Form to plan the conference for adults and teenagers.

CONFERENCE AND MEETING PLANNING FORM

Step I: Factors and Related Activities

Factors People Oriented and Task Oriented	Related Activities

1. _____   I

2. _____

3. _____

4. _____   II

5. _____

6. _____

7. _____   III

8. _____

9. _____

10. _____   IV

11. _____

12. _____

13. _____   V

14. _____

15. _____

Exercise 17.7 (Continued)

Name _____

Date _____ Hour _____

Step II: Particulars

_____

Conference Title and Theme:

Title

Theme

Other Related Aspects

_____

Conference Format:

1.

2.

3.

_____

Conference Presenters or Speakers:

1.

2.

3.

_____

Conference Place and Time:

Place

Date(s)

Hour(s)

_____

Exercise 17.7 (Continued)

Step III: Assistance Coordination

Supply here information that you feel will assist you in your work with the conference—list of individuals who will help and their possible duties, sources of materials and equipment (where and what), internal and external contacts required, (who, when, how, by whom), and other initial items that must be considered.

1.

2.

3.

4.

5.

6.

7.

8.

9.

10.

MODULE XVIII

PEER HELPING THROUGH TUTORING

Letter to say something that you never could say to person

Dear Grandpa Wentz,

I am writing you this letter to tell you how much I love you. I know in the past that it might have seemed like I didn't care much but that wasn't the case. Like the time during your last visit when you flew out but didn't see me much because of my job. I just wanted to tell you that I am very sorry and will try harder in the future not to hurt you. I Love you

Love,
David

MODULE **18**

PEER HELPING
THROUGH TUTORING

There are many problems centered around learning today:

- Falling academic standards in schools.

- Lost, lonely, and depressed students in school.

- Children who come from a different culture and can't understand others' language.

- Adults who need to learn new skills.

- Adults who are illiterate.

- Pressure to be the best.

One viable help to the above problems is through one-on-one tutoring. Research exists that supports the notion that children and adults can learn when a good relationship exists between the learner and the teacher. Additional research indicates that individuals with similar values, culture, and age (peers) can be effective in teaching others.

Tutoring is a service that is designed to aid the formal teacher. The **tutor** is the peer who is helping another in a teaching role. The **tutee** is the person receiving the service of tutoring. Generally tutoring takes place in a formal learning situation such as a school. However, it also takes place informally with friends and family.

Tutoring is a very important role that a peer can perform. It is also a very rewarding role for the tutor if the tutees learn the material being presented. The peer tutor can effectively motivate persons being tutored and effectively encourage learning in a systematic manner.

Many of the eight skills you learned in your basic training in *Peer Power: Book 1* are very important in establishing a tutoring relationship. The skill you learned in attending is important in that you need to focus on the tutees and they need to feel that you are physically with them. The skill of empathy is extremely important to be able to listen completely to tutees and hear their frustrations and problems in learning. The skill of questioning is important to learn about their present study habits. The skill of confrontation is important at times if they are not following through on an agreement they have made with you. The skill you have learned in problem solving will help you to understand how to approach others.

Motivation

How to motivate others is an important skill to know because of the role you will be playing as a tutor. When you are in the role of a tutor it is important to understand the individual needs of tutees.

The tutor must understand that individuals have very basic and very sophisticated needs. For example, if you were working with tutees who had not had anything to eat all day, they will not have satisfied their basic needs and would not be willing to spend time on a reading assignment. The tutor who understands basic needs is better able to motivate tutees.

A well-known psychologist, Abraham Maslow, developed a theory regarding human needs and motivation that is helpful in understanding personality and behavior. This is called Maslow's *Hierarchy of Needs.* The basic needs are *physiological needs,* which directly relate to survival such as food, water, air and warmth. Next are the *safety needs,* which are related to psychological safety or security and reflect a need to feel safe from outside harm. *Love needs* indicate a desire to belong and be loved and to love. *Esteem needs* include self-respect, recognition, self-esteem, stature, and attention. Finally, the higher needs are *self-actualization needs,* which involve self-fulfillment and self-growth. As a tutor you might try to decide at which level of needs you are working. For example, to be aware of lack of basic needs will be helpful to know so that you can make sure tutees have had proper food and sleep before working together. When tutees appear to have the first three satisfied, then can you motivate them to feel better about themselves?

Motivation is typically either outside the person (extrinsic) or inside the person (intrinsic). If you are working with tutees who need a great deal of outside motivation then you may want to use contracts and immediate rewards. It is known that inner motivation increases as persons begin to feel good about themselves. As a tutor, part of your job is to begin to help tutees feel good about themselves. One way is the job of encouragement.

The Art of Encouragement

When encouraging individuals, you might keep in mind a few thoughts. First, place value on individuals as they are. This can be done through good attending and empathy skills. Next show faith in them and sincerely believe in their ability to do things. Next, indicate a job that is well done and give recognition for the effort. Next, assist in the development of skills in a step-by-step process. Then recognize and focus on strengths and assets, and focus on the interests of the tutees.

Step 1. Identify the positive behaviors and traits in the tutees. You will have to spend time getting to know them as individuals, and you may want to question them on their study habits and learning styles and focus on what they are doing correctly.

Step 2. Focus on the activity and not on the person. For example, as you work with tutees, rather than saying, "You're wonderful because you got an A": It is more encouraging to say, "I really like how neat your paper is. It's much easier to read."

Step 3. Use the language of Encouragement. Some of the phrases that help tutees believe in themselves might be:

"I like how hard you worked on that problem."

"I like the way you finished that problem."

"You look pleased."

"You'll work it out."

"I have confidence in you."

"I see that you're moving along."

"You may not have reached your final goal, but look how far you've come."

"You've done a good job."

As a tutor, your job will be one of a helper, encourager, and manager. Your job is not only to relate to tutees but also to find out from the teacher exactly what the tutees need to learn; therefore you also must communicate with the professional teacher to learn what needs to be taught. Hopefully, you have the academic skills to assist the tutees; if not, then be genuine and try to find another tutor. It sounds difficult, but as a tutor you will become very aware of your own learning style; you also will begin to feel better about yourself, and you will begin to be more sensitive to others. You will begin to feel a sense of responsibility and will learn how to use your own time more efficiently.

To be an effective tutor, you must understand your own values toward helping others, your own study habits, how you learn, and then how to organize and assist others in learning.

Use. This needs to be taught only after the tutors have gone through the training in *Peer Power: Book 1*. This material is appropriate for junior high, high school, and adults to use. This module is not designed to be a complete book on tutoring. A variety of books are available on tutoring and study skills if you want to focus on more complete training. If this is the tutor's only role, additional training in tutoring is important and is recommended.

Exercise 18.1

Name _____

Date _____ Hour _____

SELF-ASSESSMENT

GOALS

This activity is designed to help you, the tutor, to assess your

1. personal characteristics for tutoring, and

2. management skills for tutoring.

Before deciding to be a tutor, it is important to do some self-assessment to see whether or not you really do have the personal characteristics and management skills to be a tutor. This assessment would be good to repeat after you have tutored others.

DIRECTIONS

1. Read the introduction to this module.

2. Respond to the "Self-Assessment Questionnaire" in this exercise.

3. Discuss with your training group and trainer your responses and complete the "Goal Sheet" for your own improvement. Then have it approved by the trainer.

4. Set your own goals for how to get yourself ready to be an effective tutor.

5. Fill out the goal sheet and bring it to the next training meeting.

Exercise 18.1 (Continued)

SELF-ASSESSMENT QUESTIONNAIRE

Please respond on a scale from 1 (Weak), 2 (Need help), 3 (Okay), 4 (Strong), 5 (Excellent). Circle the appropriate number.

	1	2	3	4	5
1. I have a lot of energy when working with people.	1	2	3	(4)	5
2. I use good attending and empathy skills when working with people.	1	2	3	4	(5)
3. I use confidentiality.	1	2	3	(4)	5
4. I am positive when working with people.	1	2	3	4	(5)
5. I have a good understanding of people and what motivates them.	1	2	(3)	4	5
6. I am creative in trying to help others.	1	2	(3)	4	5
7. I understand myself.	1	2	3	4	(5)
8. I understand my own learning style.	1	2	3	4	(5)
9. I am concerned for others.	1	2	3	4	(5)
10. I am good at managing my own time.	1	2	(3)	4	5
11. I am self-disciplined.	1	2	3	(4)	5
12. I am self-confident.	1	2	3	(4)	5
13. I like to learn.	1	2	3	(4)	5
14. I enjoy school.	1	2	(3)	4	5
15. I can finish things that I follow through with.	1	2	3	(4)	5
16. I can set goals.	1	2	3	4	(5)
17. I can motivate others.	1	2	(3)	4	5
18. I can keep records of attendance and what has been learned.	1	2	3	4	(5)

Exercise 18.1 (Continued)   Name _David Luwenga_

                                        Date _____ Hour _____

19. I can talk with the professional teacher about a specific
    student and specific skill to be learned.   1   2   3   4   (5)

20. I can use encouraging statements with the tutee.   1   2   3   4   (5)

21. I can help the tutee get the correct answer.   1   2   3   (4)   5

22. I have the academic skills needed to help the tutee.   1   2   3   4   (5)

23. I have patience while working with others.   1   2   (3)   4   5

24. I have a good sense of humor while working with others.   1   2   3   (4)   5

25. I am good at having the right materials needed for tutoring. 1   2   3   (4)   5

26. I am good at planning ahead of time what needs to be done
    during the tutoring time (setting goals, activities, materials). 1 2 (3)   4   5

27. I am good at giving positive feedback to the tutee.   1   2   3   (4)   5

28. I can keep the tutee on task.   1   2   3   4   (5)

29. I have good attendance.   1   2   3   4   (5)

SCORING

Directions: Add the circled numbers to obtain a total score.

    30-60   Get help from the trainer in weak areas before starting to tutor.

    60-120   Go ahead and start tutoring, but get help in weak areas.   (121)

    120-150   Go become a professional teacher.

Discussion

    1. Look at the statements for which you circled 1 or 2 and share these with the group.

    2. Have the group help you in setting goals to improve these areas.

Exercise 18.1 (Continued)

1. My strengths as a tutor are

    My knowledge of material

    my ability to communicate with tutee

2. My weaknesses as a tutor are

    my patients sometimes

    managing time

3. My goal to improve my weaknesses is

    work them through by helping others

    and keeping those in my mind while

    helping that person

4. My plan to accomplish the goal is as follows:

    - Who is needed?

        a student to tutor

    - What I need to do?

        keep focused on my task

    - When?

        whenever possible

        (as soon as possible)

5. Evaluation

_____

Trainer approval

_____

Peer tutor signature

Exercise 18.2

Name _~David Lurney~_

Date _____ Hour _____

HOW I STUDY

GOALS

In this exercise you will learn

1. to understand your own study habits, and

2. to improve your own study habits.

DIRECTIONS

1. Read and answer the questions on the *"Personal Study Habits Survey."*

2. Rate yourself.

3. Set some goals and develop a plan on how you can improve.

4. Use the *"Personal Study Habits Survey"* with your tutor once you have established rapport.

PERSONAL STUDY HABITS SURVEY

Yes	No		
✓		1.	Do you have a regular schedule for study, a particular time to save for study?
✓		2.	Do you frequently have a radio, record, or the television playing as you study?
✓		3.	Do you have a regular place to study?
	✓	4.	Is your study often interrupted by telephoning, visiting, looking at magazines, or other activities?
	✓	5.	Do you try to be fresh and rested for studying, not putting it off or scheduling it when you are tired from other activities?
	✓	6.	Do you usually sit in an easy chair or lie down to study?
✓		7.	Do you begin the study of a topic by quickly glancing over the topic to see what it is about?

Exercise 18.2 (Continued)

Yes / No

___✓___ ___ 8. Do you always read a topic or chapter before reading the summary (if there is one) at the end?

___ ___✓___ 9. Do you always try to "think through" a topic and decide what you are supposed to learn from it rather than just reading it over in studying?

___ ___✓___ 10. Do you have difficulty in concentrating fully when you are studying?

___✓___ ___ 11. Do you concentrate fully when you are studying?

___ ___✓___ 12. Do you seldom review except just before tests?

___✓___ ___ 13. As you study, do you constantly try to express in your own words what the author is saying?

___✓___ ___ 14. Do you review by rereading or scanning the material that you are to be tested on?

___✓___ ___ 15. Do you review some of each subject that you have studied on a previous day as well as studying new material?

___✓___ ___ 16. Do you try to do the exact assignment that your teacher has given?

___✓___ ___ 17. Do you take a great many notes on what the teacher says?

___✓___ ___ 18. Do you seldom take notes on reading assignments?

___ ___✓___ 19. Do you put notes in outline form as soon after taking them as possible?

___ ___✓___ 20. Do you have difficulty "making sense" of your notes when you study them later?

___✓___ ___ 21. In reviewing, do you read a note and then try to remember all the details that went with it?

___ ___✓___ 22. Do you rewrite all your notes?

___✓___ ___ 23. During lectures, do you look at the instructor when you are not taking notes?

___ ___✓___ 24. Are you relaxed and take it easy in class?

___✓___ ___ 25. Do you think about what the instructor is saying as well as listening to what he says?

___ ___✓___ 26. Do you often find that you are studying with only "half of your mind"—or even less?

Name _____

Date _____ Hour _____

Yes	No		
✓	___	27.	Do you often try to figure out whether or not the subject you are studying may be helpful to you later in life?
✓	___	28.	Do you believe that, if you were to learn each paragraph of a chapter well, you would have learned the chapter well?
✓	___	29.	Do you try to fit all you read on a subject into a big, overall idea or mental picture of the subject?
___	✓	30.	Sometimes when studying do you seem to get lost in details—you "can't see the forest for the trees"?
✓	___	31.	Do you believe that in addition to learning the details of a subject you must learn the big, overall story or idea of the subject?
✓	___	32.	Do you customarily read at the speed that is easy and most natural for you?
___	✓	33.	Do you often tell yourself when studying, "I'm going to remember this especially!"?
✓	___	34.	Do you not know how to increase your speed in reading?
✓	___	35.	Do you deliberately study and plan to be able to participate in a class discussion?
✓	___	36.	Do you do a little extra studying before tests?
✓	___	37.	Do you think through the meaning of test questions before you begin to answer them?
✓	___	38.	Do you stay up late the night before a test, studying for it?
___	✓	39.	On an essay-type test, do you outline your answers before beginning to write them?
✓	___	40.	Do you suspect that many test questions are tricky, designed to fool you rather than test your knowledge?
✓	___	41.	Are you willing to work harder during the time you spend?

Scoring

Give yourself a point for every odd number (1, 3, 5, 7, etc.) that you answered YES, and one point for every even number (2, 4, 6, 8, etc.) that you answer NO.

Record your score on the *"My Rank on Study Skills"* chart and observe the face reflection of your score.

WHERE DO YOU RANK?

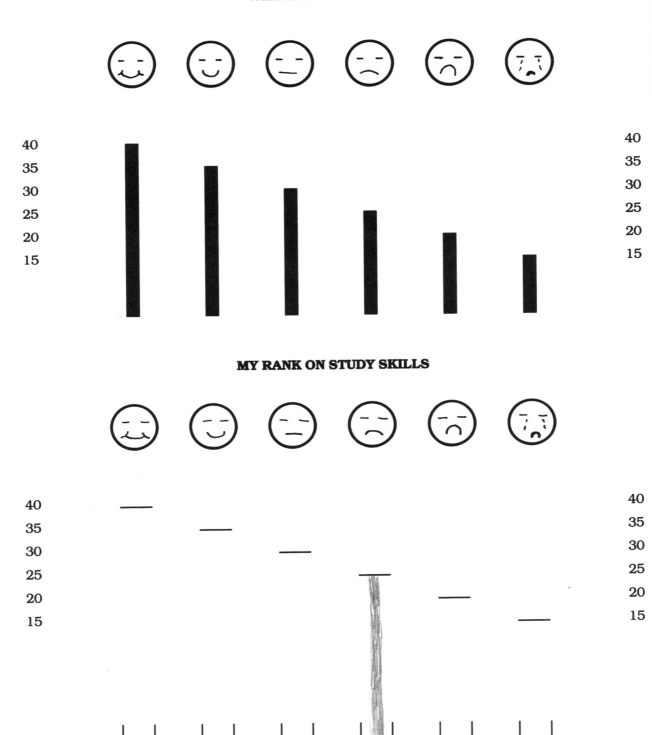

MY RANK ON STUDY SKILLS

Exercise 18.3

Name _____

Date _____ Hour _____

HOW I LEARN BEST

GOALS

In this exercise you will learn

1. your preferred way of learning,

2. how this affects your approach to study, and

3. how learning styles can help you as a tutor.

DIRECTIONS

1. Take the *"Learning Style Survey"* to assess how you prefer to learn and how you prefer to show what you have learned.

2. Score the survey

3. Respond to the discussion questions.

4. Design how you would tutor a person who learns best by the following.

   a. Visually

   b. Auditorially

   c. Kinesthetically

5. Identify how would you use this information to teach skills in reading, math, test preparation, and writing papers.

LEARNING STYLE SURVEY

What is the best manner of learning for you? Often it is obvious in babies in that they can understand best by watching things or sometimes hearing things or sometimes feeling things. We all have a preferred way of learning. This does not mean that we cannot learn by other means, but if we know our preferred way of learning, if we are approaching a difficult task, then the preferred procedure is to use our best learning mode. We also need to develop other ways of learning.

The visual learner prefers to learn by watching and reading. The auditory learner prefers to learn by listening. The kinesthetic learner prefers to learn best by doing something.

Exercise 18.3 (Continued)

1. During your leisure time, which do you prefer to do?

   a. Read

   b. Listen to the radio

   c. Be active by playing a game

2. If you were going to choose only one activity to join, which would it be?

   a. Reading club

   b. Public speaking club

   c. Drama

3. During your class, which would you prefer to do?

   a. Look at pictures

   b. Listen to a speaker

   c. Do something active (paint, run).

4. How would you imagine something?

   a. Visually see the scene.

   b. Listen to what is happening in the scene.

   c. Feel movement or sensations in the scene.

5. When you walk into a gathering of friends, which do you do?

   a. Look around and see what is happening.

   b. Talk to someone.

   c. Try to actively do something.

6. What do you remember best?

   a. An individual's face

   b. Things people tell you

   c. Activities you have done

7. When you are trying to learn something new, which do you do most?

   a. Look at it carefully

   b. Say it out loud

   c. Write it a few times

Exercise 18.3 (Continued)

Name _____

Date _____ Hour _____

8. What assignment would you prefer?

   a. Read a book

   b. Give a speech

   (c.) Make a project

9. When you study, which do you prefer?

   a. A neat desk

   (b.) Things to be very quiet

   c. The place to be very comfortable.

10. If you needed to get information, how would you prefer to get it?

   (a.) In writing

   b. By phone

   c. Through something you would have to put together

Scoring

How many A's did you circle? _____3_____

How many B's did you circle? _____2_____

How many C's did you circle? _____5_____

Code:

A means that you might learn best by watching. Your visual ability is your best way to learn.

B means that you learn best by listening. Your style of learning is more auditory.

C means that you learn best by doing. You probably learn best by a kinesthetic activity.

Exercise 18.3 (Continued)

Discussion Questions

1. Which style is preferred?

> Kinesthetic - to learn something by actually doing it.

2. If you must learn something, what is your preferred manner?

> a little of each

3. How can you use this information in studying?

> use the information given then change it to my preferred method of studying.

4. How can you use this information in tutoring?

> when you find out what kind of person your tutoring you can use this method to help him/her learn better

Exercise 18.4

Name _____

Date _____ Hour _____

MAJOR STUDY SKILLS

GOALS

This activity will help you to learn techniques

1. for tutoring in reading, writing, note taking, and test taking; and

2. for ways to apply these skills in a tutoring situation.

DIRECTIONS

1. Read the information contained in this exercise. This information may be used by you to help your tutee on how to learn.

2. Develop strategies for using one of these skills to help your tutee.

3. Divide into groups consisting of three members—one as tutor, one as tutee, and one as observer. Then role play three of the following examples, changing roles after each role playing and receiving feedback from the observer.

   a. Work with a person who plays the role of a tutee who cannot retain what they have read. Work with the tutee to teach the SQ3R method.

   b. Work with a person who plays the role of a tutee who has difficulty taking notes.

   c. Work with a person who plays the role of a tutee who has a difficult time in time management.

   d. Work with a person who plays the role of a tutee who has a difficult time in note taking.

   e. Work with a person who plays the role of a tutee who has a difficult time in theme writing.

4. Identify those areas in which you need some help so that you can help others.

5. Specify additional techniques that you may use in these areas to be helpful to tutees.

6. Design an approach to assist someone who is trying to study for a test:

   a. Visual learner

   b. Auditory learner

   c. Kinesthetic learner

7. Develop a plan to help someone develop good note-taking skills.

8. Develop a plan to help someone develop good reading and memory skills.

9. Note the differences in your two plans developed numbers 7 and 8.

READING—SQ3R

The SQ3R method of reading is a technique that will help you remember what you have read. For example, if you are reading an important note from your best friend, you can remember everything about it without concentrating. You do not need to underline or outline to remember. Reading required work is different; you need to learn techniques that will help you to remember what you have read. The SQ3R technique is best.

Survey

1. Examine the title of each chapter.

2. Note headings and subheadings and the relationship among important headings in each chapter.

3. Glance at the diagrams, graphs, and visuals.

4. Quickly skim the introductory and concluding sections.

5. Notice summary statements and questions or activities.

Question

Begin each section of a chapter and ask the following questions:

1. Who?
2. What?
3. When?
4. Where?
5. How?

Turn each heading into a question.

Read and Underline

Read each section with the question in mind and go back and mark or underline the important material. You may have to read the material several times before you are able to highlight the essential material.

1. Do not highlight or underline the first time you read.

2. Use vertical lines in the margin to emphasize main points.

3. Circle important concepts.

4. Highlight the points underlined.

5. Practice the skill.

Exercise 18.4 (Continued)

Name _____

Date _____ Hour _____

Recite and Write Study Notes

Once you have formed questions and underlined well, recite the answers to your questions out loud or write them. Also, write brief study notes. Write a summary sentence of the main idea in each paragraph if the material is extremely difficult for you.

Review The Entire Chapter

Once you have read the entire chapter, you are ready to review:

1. Reread the main headings.

2. Review the underlined and highlighted items.

3. Review the answer to the questions you had formed for each section.

TEST TAKING

FIVE EASY STEPS
FOR IMPROVING TEST SCORES

When taking a test several things can be done to help make test taking easier and to help you achieve higher scores. Here are five simple steps that, when followed, can help ensure a better chance for success:

1. **Preview the test.** Look over, or preview, the entire test before answering any questions. By doing this, you will get a quick idea of what the test is all about.

2. **Arrange your time.** Find out how many points each question is worth. Some questions might be worth more than others. You'll want to make especially sure that you do the questions of higher value. If the test contains easy questions, make sure to allow enough time to complete them.

3. **Look for clue words.** Be aware of and look for words that tell you what type of question you are answering. Here are some clue words to look for on tests.

   a. In the following example, the word "an" is a clue word telling you the "b" is the correct answer:

      a. _____ conversation
      b. _____ oration
      c. _____ talk
      d. _____ trembling

      The word "an" is used only before words that begin with a vowel (a, e, i, o, u). Answers "a," "c," and "d" do not begin with vowels; therefore "oration" has to be the correct answer.

   b. There are important clue words to look for on true/false tests also. Words such as "all," "always," "never," and "none" have no exceptions. Very often, but not always, these clue words tell you that the statement is false. Clue words such as "many," "may," "some," and "might" leave room for some exceptions. These words are often clues that the statement is true. Examine these examples:

      T F   All police officers are men

      T F   Some police officers are women

   c. The clue words on essay tests tell you exactly what you have to do. Watch for them: define, explain, outline, describe, compare, discuss.

4. **Answer the easy questions first.** Previewing the test (Step 1) helps you with this step. Do all the questions for which you know the answers first, while perhaps making a mark next to those items that you are not sure about. After doing the questions you know, go back to the ones that you skipped. By doing this simple procedure, you have made sure that you have completed those answers you could answer in the event that you do not finish the test. On essay tests, this test step is perhaps even more important.

Name _____

Date _____ Hour _____

5. Review the test before handing it to your teacher. Look over your test when you have finished. You may find some careless mistakes. When reviewing an essay test, consider these questions:

    a. Did you write what you really meant?

    b. Did you really answer what the questions asked?

    c. Are your answers clear? (Is it obvious what you are trying to say?)

    d. Did you follow the directions and answer all the questions to the best of your ability?

TEST YOUR TEST-TAKING SKILLS

Points

Points	
10	1. The five vowels are _a_ _e_ _i_ _o_ _u_
10	2. A consonant that is sometimes used as a vowel is _y_
15	3. There can never be a vowel sound in a word without a vowel letter. _____ T __X__ F
15	4. How many syllables does the word "equitable" have? _4_

Write the meaning of each word below:

5	5. Innocent __free of blame__
5	6. Erroneous __magnificent , exaggerated__
10	7. Enfranchisement _____

Divide these words into syllables:

10	8. Escape __Es cape__
10	9. Engrave __En grave__
10	10. Inopportune __In op por tune__

10-point bonus: write a three-syllable word and its definition:

__penalty - effect of doing a wrong action ; punishment__

_____

_____

ESSAY-TYPE EXAMINATIONS

1. Glance over the test. Check the number of questions. Decide how much time you should allow for each (30 seconds should be enough for this task of budgeting time).

2. Look at the first question. What does it ask you to do? Compare? Contrast? Discuss? Define? Trace? Explain? Outline? List? Each of these means something different. Make sure that you understand for what the question calls.

3. On a piece of scratch paper organize your ideas and outline what you are going to say.

4. If you finish before time, go back and see if anything can be added. Look for misspelled words, grammatical errors, etc. This may mean the difference between passing and failing.

5. Write neatly.

6. Give examples to support your ideas.

TRUE-FALSE TESTS

1. True-false tests present a new type of situation. This means that you must use extreme care in the reading of each individual statement. Be sure that you know what it says.

2. True-false tests usually contain several questions. No one question can, therefore, be of too great an importance. Answer each question to the best of your knowledge and forget it.

3. Give your full attention to each question.

4. If you have time, go back and try a new approach. What was said about this in class? What did the instructor say about this? Changes made under these conditions have proved to be consistently from "wrong" to "right" answers.

5. Be leary of any true-false questions that have "always" or "never" in them. Usually they are false.

MULTIPLE-CHOICE TESTS

1. These are tricky; be sure to read correctly each part of the question.

2. Give each question your full attention.

3. First read and study the question thoroughly. Know what is being asked and what sort of an answer is required.

4. Only after careful study of the questions, and while holding this in mind, should you look at the proposed alternate responses.

5. Relax between each question for a few seconds so that you will be fresh for the next question.

PROBLEM-SOLVING TESTS

1. Study the problem, analyze the problem. Ask yourself: "What did the teacher ask in this problem?" "Which of the principles that we have studied could be used in the solution of this kind of problem?" "What are the steps to be used in the solution?" "How are these steps written?" This thinking in words will help you to select the correct process.

2. Use proper notations and write solutions as completely as possible. If you leave out steps, you will have to go through them when checking, and this may lead to mistakes and may cause error.

3. Keep thinking in words about what you are doing as you work out the solution. This helps keep your mind centered on the task and helps to avoid errors in method.

4. When finished, relax and go back through test checking, reasoning, arithmetic, and algebraic signs (not necessarily math problems).

THEME WRITING AND NOTE TAKING

Effective expression is important now and will be an asset in any occupation. Some of the following suggestions may be helpful in making your note taking more enjoyable.

1. Select a topic of interest to you.

2. Make it specific enough to find information about the subject.

3. Make it worth writing about.

4. Make it important enough to you to be worth writing about.

Have an outline or plan of what you are going to write. It is much easier to change an outline than to change a theme after it is written.

Gather information from different sources and put the information on slips of paper for notes.

Find the central thought in each group and then expand the idea with examples, comparisons, contrasts, and analogies.

Arrange the ideas in logical sequence.

Select words that are suited best to your meaning.

Revise the sentence structure and word choice.

Let your theme rest for a time, then read it and find the mistakes—e.g., spelling.

Accurate, readable notes are invaluable aids during high school and in later life. Notes should be taken during lectures, textbook reading sessions, discussions. The keynote of good note taking is to listen much and write little. Learn to identify main points and ideas and write them out in outline form.

Exercise 18.4 (Continued)

1. Use an 8-½ x 11 notebook preferably. Use dividers to separate the various subjects. Keep notes on one subject together.

2. Strive to take good notes the first time. Do not plan to recopy notes; recopy only when clarity and conciseness demand it.

3. Doodling is bound to distract your attention; avoid it.

4. Review your notes for about five minutes the same day you take them and at least once a week for about an hour at a planned time.

5. Take down accurately any assignment. If you do not understand the assignment, ask the teacher.

ORGANIZE YOUR TIME

In school you will need to budget your time more carefully than you have done before. To gain balance among your daily activities, you must know that basically there are several specific activities for which you must allow time:

1. You must sleep: one needs 7 or 8 hours of uninterrupted sleep to enable one to carry on the other 16 or 17 hours of waking time.

2. You must eat (three meals a day).

3. You must allow time for personal grooming.

4. You must attend classes.

5. You must study.

Make a reasonable schedule and stick to it. A suggested time chart form is shown following. Construct your own and use it.

Study periods should be about 50 minutes long for maximum effectiveness. If you need to study longer, "take a break" after about 50 minutes and then resume study.

Use time in class for study. Most students are most efficient during the day when the assignment is fresh in their mind. If you must earn money, schedule the type of classes that require little homework. School is a full-time job, so you should not try to carry a heavy schedule and work also. Your grades will follow you the rest of your life. Therefore, make your grades be good grades.

Name _____

Date _____   Hour _____

SAMPLE DAILY SCHEDULE

	Monday	Tuesday	Wednesday	Thursday	Friday	Saturday	Sunday
2:00 - 2:30	School					homework	homework
2:30 - 3:30	homework					work	
3:30 - 4:30	work						
4:30 - 5:30							
5:30 - 6:30							youth
6:30 - 7:30							
7:30 - 8:30							homework
8:30 - 9:30							
9:30 - 10:30	homework					social time	

Name —————

Date ————— Hour —————

YOUR OWN DAILY SCHEDULE

	Monday	Tuesday	Wednesday	Thursday	Friday	Saturday	Sunday
2:00 - 2:30							
2:30 - 3:30							
3:30 - 4:30							
4:30 - 5:30							
5:30 - 6:30							
6:30 - 7:30							
7:30 - 8:30							
8:30 - 9:30							
9:30 - 10:30							

Exercise 18.5

PROBLEMS IN TUTORING

GOALS

In this exercise you will learn

1. to apply skills learned to problem areas in tutoring, and

2. to practice using skills in tutoring.

DIRECTIONS

1. Work with a partner and practice the following:

Tutee: Looks angry

Response:

Tutee: "Sue keeps making fun of me on my low scores on the math test. I feel like telling her off!"

Response:

Tutee: "I just failed another test in history. I can't seem to understand the book."

Response:

Tutee: "You had this class, you know what to do."

Response:

2. Work with a partner and role play the following three situations with "encouragement" being given by the tutor. (This may be combined with Direction 4.)

   a. A student complains that homework is too difficult and too extensive.

   b. A tutee is afraid to give a speech in class.

   c. A tutee plays a game well but lost.

3. In role playing construct a contract with the tutee on note taking. Use the *"Sample Note-taking Contract."*

4. Role play setting up positive reinforcers for completion of either situation 2a or 2b.

5. Write a confrontation statement for the following situation:

   You have been working with the tutee for several weeks and know her well. Recently she has been uncooperative and not wanting to work with you. She says that she wants to do better in math but continues to play around during her tutoring session.

Exercise 18.5 (Continued)

Confrontation statement: _____

_____

_____

_____

6. Write several encouraging statements that you might use in tutoring situations.

SAMPLE NOTE-TAKING CONTRACT

NAME: John

BEGINNING DATE: 2/4   **ENDING DATE:**   2/8

INSTRUCTOR'S NOTE:

When John writes at least a half page of notes each day in World History, then he will be able to bring his favorite music to the next tutoring session.

_____

John

_____

Tutor

Exercise 18.6

PUTTING TUTORING SKILLS INTO ACTION

GOAL

This activity will help you as a peer helper

1. to learn the steps involved in your role as a successful tutor, and

2. to practice tutoring.

DIRECTIONS

1. Review with participants concepts and work from Exercise 18.5.

2. Read the *"Steps Involved in Successful Tutoring."*

3. Write *"Your Plan for Working with Your Tutee."*

4. Discuss the plan with the leader.

5. Role play tutoring by asking someone to be a tutee, another person to be an observer, and you play the tutor. The role of the tutor is to role play the first meeting with the tutee. Have the observer to complete the *"Observation Sheet."*

6. If you feel prepared to be a tutor, meet with your cooperating teacher and obtain a tutee assignment.

STEPS INVOLVED IN SUCCESSFUL TUTORING

Step One

1. Understand the overall organizational structure of your tutoring assignment.

   a. Your facilitator/coordinator will train you and help you to organize your tutoring time and find a location in which to do tutoring.

   b. Your cooperating teacher will provide you with the tutee and the materials needed to do tutoring and the specific skill needed.

   c. Learn where you are to do the tutoring and how much time you have to teach the skill. Keep attendance on the tutee.

2. Keep in mind that you have your own values and attitudes about learning and studying. Be sure that you do not put down the tutee if they are different than your's.

3. Know your tutee before you begin working on a skill. Try to spend time learning about the tutee's interests, listening to descriptions of family, friends, and so forth.

Exercise 18.6 (Continued)

Step Two

4. Keep regular contact with the tutee's teacher.

5. Focus on the tutee, using your best attending skills.

6. Listen completely (use good empathy).

7. Establish trust by keeping it confidential that you are tutoring the person.

8. Use the language of encouragement.

9. Be respectful toward the tutee.

10. Make sure the tutee understands your role and the purpose of the time together.

11. Appear as relaxed as possible.

12. Have the material ready (paper, pencil, correct books, etc.).

13. Use the correct language, vocabulary, pronunciation of the subject.

14. Help tutees if they are struggling by giving them the answers.

15. Don't be afraid to be human, for example, don't be afraid to tell them, "I don't know."

16. Be a positive peer model by following the rules yourself.

17. Do not criticize your tutee or their teacher.

18. Stay enthusiastic throughout the meeting.

19. When your time is completed, review what has been learned and compliment them for their hard work.

Step Three

20. Have a plan for the first time you meet the tutee:

   a. Establish a warm, relaxed, pleasant atmosphere; attend to the tutee, have materials, smile, and be pleasant.

   b. Begin the meeting with pleasant conversation, asking about the tutee's interest and say something about yourself.

   c. Find out how the tutee learns best; discuss.

   d. Find out how the tutee studies best; discuss.

   e. Make sure that you have all the materials.

Exercise 18.6 (Continued)

Name _____

Date _____ Hour _____

    f.   Explain your role and the work to be learned.

    g.   Use positive reinforcers and encouraging statements.

    h.   Give them feedback for that day.

    i.   Set up a time and place for the next meeting.

YOUR PLAN FOR WORKING WITH YOUR TUTEE

After reading the *"Steps Involved in Successful Tutoring,"* think of a person whom you will be tutoring in the future. Write your plan for working with the tutee.

1. Preparing

2. Learning about the tutee.

3. Establishing rapport.

4. Working with supervising teacher.

5. Subject matter tutoring

6. Some positive remarks.

7. Some encouraging statements.

8. How are you going to deal with problems?

Discuss your plan with your facilitator/supervisor.

OBSERVATION SHEET

	High	Medium	Low	Comments
Attending behavior				
Empathy				
Heard meaning and feeling				
Rapport with the person				
Positive reinforcement				
Encouraging words				
Provided structure for the meeting				
Got to know tutee				
Good role model				
Respect				
Confidentiality				
Other				

MODULE XIX

FACILITATING SMALL DISCUSSION GROUPS

FACILITATING SMALL DISCUSSION GROUPS

Discussion skills can be used with small groups in a variety of settings. They can be used in schools for one of the prevention approaches to substance abuse, sexuality issues, health issues, value clarification, and so forth. Discussion groups have been used in business in "quality circles" to help employees be more involved in the business and assist the business in higher productivity and profit. In organizations in all settings (school, church, agency, business) groups are often used to help individuals make decisions concerning different issues. Research indicates that group decisions are often better and more creative than are individual decisions. Sometimes organizations have "rap groups," where the focus is more on what the group wants to discuss. There is no set curriculum or message, there is no decision that must be made. The rap group approach has been used to assist group members in solving problems in their daily lives.

Generally a good discussion leads toward a better group product than that which an individual might initiate. Group discussion often leads to one reexamining own feelings. It also teaches listening skills to participants and develops better interpersonal relationships. At times, group discussion can lead to problem solving. Individuals are often more able to deal with controversial matters in a group discussion as well as with persons of different backgrounds.

Pitfalls do exist in a discussion group, for example, when facilitators try to impose their own ideas. At times this is appropriate—when it is a specific subject. Sometimes the group experience becomes a free for all, and at times, when a quick decision is needed, the group experience takes too long.

Before starting this module review your basic skills because they will be needed to facilitate groups effectively. For example, the skill of **attending** is needed so that the group participants feel that the facilitator is interested in them. The skill of **empathy** is needed to hear accurately what each person is saying. The skill of **summarization** is important in terms of capturing the essence of what is being said in different words with the effect of adding meaning or clarifying meaning. **Questioning** is important to stimulate thought and action and to avoid a question/answer pattern between the facilitator and the group members.

The skill of **genuineness** often is very facilitative in a group, especially when the facilitator can share how they are feeling in terms of how they feel relative to the here-and-now occurrences in the group. **Confrontation** at times is important for challenging the members in a direct way on discrepancies in such a manner that they will tend to react nondefensively to the confrontation. The use of **assertiveness** is important infrequently to bring order to the group and more toward resolution. If the group's purpose is to problem solve and come up with a decision, then the skills of **problem-solving** are important.

The skill of facilitating a small group discussion is obviously a combination of skills that can be used in a variety of settings. As a facilitator you need to understand the purpose of the group. Is it to facilitate a rap group? Facilitate a topical group? Facilitate a problem-solving group to complete a task? or If for some other purpose, what? Think in terms of which of the three classifications the small group discussion is—**open-ended,** (e.g., life problems group), **specific topic** (e.g., subject matter group), or **task** (e.g., problem-solving group).

Use. This module could be used along with the Leadership Module. Many of the group projects of the peer counselor need to have this training before starting the projects. This can be used with junior high through adult and senior citizen levels.

Exercise 19.1

Name _____

Date _____ Hour _____

SELF-ASSESSMENT OF
GROUP FACILITATOR SKILLS

GOALS

In this exercise you will learn

1. how you view your own group facilitator skills, and

2. to set some personal goals to enhance your basic skills.

DIRECTIONS

1. Take the assessment entitled *"Checking Skill Levels"* to help you to understand your strengths as a group facilitator as well as specific areas that you need to improve.

2. Read the brief description next to each skill and then rate yourself.

3. Think about the questions listed under each skill. These will help you to determine your level of skill development and examine your behavior as a facilitator. Ask yourself what you need to develop.

4. Divide into small groups and discuss within your group the skills and how you can improve yours. Also help others in the group to improve theirs.

5. Following the discussion in the group, complete the form entitled *"My Self-Assessment of Group Facilitator Skills."*

6. Be a participant in a discussion group and observe the leader in terms of skills identified in the *"Checking Skill Levels"* instrument.

7. Participate in the discussion as a facilitator and check your skill levels on the issues.

8. Consider using the *"Checking Skill Levels"* instrument following each session during which you facilitate a group and reviewing it before you facilitate the group.

CHECKING SKILL LEVELS

Key   3—I do this most of the time with high competence.
          2—I do this some of the time with average competence.
          1—I do this rarely with low competence.

_____   1. **Attending.** Completely focusing on the group. The body language of the facilitator is tuned in to the group.

  a. How well do you have eye contact with the group?
  b. How open is your body language to the group?
  c. How able are you to mirror some of the expression of the group members?
  d. How well are you able to model attending skills as the different individuals talk?

_____   2. **Empathy.** Helping others to understand by listening accurately to others in the group so that they feel understood in terms of the content of their message and their feelings.

  a. How able are you to reflect accurately feelings?
  b. How able are you to reflect accurately content?
  c. Do your reflections help members to clarify what they are feeling and thinking?

_____   3. **Summarization.** Explaining the meaning of the message within a different context.

  a. How able are you to pull the loose ends together?
  b. Are you able to tie the various themes together for the group?
  c. Are you able to summarize what more than one person said?

_____   4. **Pulling the Group Together.** The ability to link group members together.

  a. How able are you to demonstrate that two individuals are similar?
  b. How able are you to get the group members to help each other?
  c. How able are you to get the group members to volunteer to talk?
  d. How able are you to get the group members comfortable with each other?

_____   5. **Questioning.** The ability to ask "How?" "What?" "Would?" kinds of questions.

  a. Were the questions open-ended?
  b. Did the questions help to clarify the issue?
  c. Did the questions facilitate the group toward understanding and problem solving?

_____   6. **Genuineness.** Willingness to share with members' personal feelings about the group and behavior.

  a. Were you able to identify your feelings during the group session?
  b. Were you able to share your feelings with the group?
  c. Were you able to model appropriate self-disclosure?
  d. What impact does your genuineness have on the group?

Name _____

Date _____ Hour _____

___ 7. **Confrontation.** Challenging members in a direct way that points out discrepancies.

   a. How did you confront members?
   b. Were you sensitive to timing the confrontation?
   c. Was the confrontation about specific behavior rather than judgments?
   d. Did the confrontation facilitate the group?

___ 8. **Assertiveness.** This is the ability to state how you feel about specific behavior of the group and moving them to more productive behavior.

   a. Were you able to redirect inappropriate behavior?
   b. Were you able to move the group toward a decision?
   c. Were you able to stick with the norms of the group and did the group stick with the norms?

___ 9. **Problem-Solving.** Resolution of an issue or completing a task.

   a. Were you able to help the group to explore the problem?
   b. Were you able to help the group to brainstorm solutions?
   c. Were you able to help the group to examine possible solutions?
   d. Were you able to help the group to come up with the best solution?
   e. Were you able to help the group to put the solution into action?

___ 10. **Group Control.** The ability to intervene when a group member behaves inappropriately to another group member.

   a. Were you able to keep the group on task?
   b. Were you able to redirect inappropriate behavior?
   c. Were you able to block counterproductive behavior in a firm manner?

___ 11. **Starting and Ending the Group.**

   a. Were you able to set a comfortable stage for the group?
   b. Were you able to help the group members to know each other?
   c. Was the climate of the group healthy?
   d. Did you help to bring the group to a close?

___ 12. **Guidelines for the Group.** The opportunity for the facilitator and group members to set up guidelines when appropriate.

   a. Were you able to establish a code of confidentiality?
   b. Were you able to establish the goal of the group?
   c. Were you able to get all of the group members to participate?
   d. Were you able to complete the task, lesson, or goal?

Exercise 19.1 (Continued)

MY SELF-ASSESSMENT OF
GROUP FACILITATOR SKILLS

1. My strengths are

2. My weaknesses are

3. I need more help in

Exercise 19.2

FUNCTIONS OF A DISCUSSION FACILITATOR

GOALS

In this exercise you will learn

1. the functions of a facilitator, and

2. the different issues of facilitating a group.

INTRODUCTION

Often individuals who first start facilitating groups are unaware of some basic activities needed to assure the success of a group. This exercise will help you as a facilitator to focus on those activities.

DIRECTIONS

1. Look at the list of *"Group Facilitator Functions"* and add any further ideas.

2. Discuss fully, based on your own personal experiences, any additional ideas.

3. Move into small groups of four, each with one observer; have each group take only one of the issues in *"Group Facilitator Functions,"* and role play a group activity. Change roles so that each group member leads, participates, and observes.

4. Use the feedback form entitled *"Discussion Skills Observation"* facilitator. Discuss skill of the observer.

5. Look at the other observation factors.

   a. Was the atmosphere relaxed?

   b. Did the members all participate?

   c. Who is being left out?

   d. How does the group affect the facilitator?

   e. Does the outline affect or help or hinder?

6. Look at the checklist in Exercise 19.1 and evaluate your own effectiveness in each situation.

Exercise 19.2 (Continued)

GROUP FACILITATOR FUNCTIONS

1. Establishing the Climate

   a. Make sure that you know the purpose of the group.
   b. If materials are needed, please have them prepared.
   c. Check the room for comfort—ventilation, lighting, and seats placed in a circle.
   d. Introduce the group members either through name tags, brief introductions, or other means.
   e. Try to have the introductions relate to the purpose of the group.

2. Clarifying the Topic for Discussion

   a. If you have established a topic, write it on the board.
   b. If it is open-ended, write this on the board.
   c. If it is a task group or problem-solving group, write the task or problem on the board.
   d. If there is an agenda, write it on the board.
   e. Make sure that the purpose is clear to the group members.

3. Norms of the Group

   a. Discuss the norms that the group wants.
   b. Confidentiality.
   c. Recording information.
   d. Participation.
   e. Being drug free.
   f. If the group is expected to make a report, ask for a volunteer to write the notes.
   g. Listen to each other.
   h. Other.

4. Statements with Which to Open the Meeting After Introductions

   a. "What do you want from today's group meeting?"
   b. "Last time we left off here _____.
      What reactions do you have about it?"
   c. "Did anyone think about anything after the last time?"
   d. "I would like everyone to complete this sentence:
      'Right now I am feeling _____.'"
   e. "I would like to share some of my thoughts and feelings about the last group meeting."
   f. "Could we have a report about the progress of the group?"
   g. "Do you have any issues that you would like to pursue?"
   h. Additional phrases.

5. Dealing with Difficult Group Members

   a. Dominating.

      (1) Offer privately feedback to a dominating person.
      (2) Suggest privately ways for the dominating person to contribute without taking over the group.

172   *Peer Power: Book 2*

Name _____

Date _____ Hour _____

(3) Ask directly questions of other group members.
(4) Begin your discussion with comments of other group members.
(5) Break in on long comments by dominating the person; thank them for their ideas and then elicit comments from others.

b. Hypercritical.

(1) Emphasize the importance of considering all ideas.
(2) Emphasize the importance of respectful communication.
(3) Recognize the value of the content of the criticism (if honest), but disapprove of how the criticism was stated.
(4) Offer feedback to the hypercritical person.
(5) Encourage criticisms to be stated specifically, with suggestions for alternative approaches.
(6) Remind the members that they can "get along" for the short time the sessions will last.

c. Silent members—Call on them, ignore them, pay attention to nonverbal messages.
d. Monopolizer—Talk privately, confrontation.
e. Storytelling—Genuineness, stick to agenda.
f. Angry member.
g. Blocker.
h. Joking, assertiveness. "Now, let's get down to business."
i. Other.

6. Suggestions for Closing the Group

a. "Before we end today, is there anything anyone would want to say?"
b. "What did you learn today about _____?"
c. "If each of you could summarize the point of the group, what would it be?"
d. "Please complete this sentence: One thing I need to practice outside of the group this week is _____."
e. "Please complete this sentence: My assignment is _____."
f. "Does anyone want to give any feedback?"
g. "Are there any changes that you would like to suggest for next time?"
h. "How do you feel about the decisions that we made?"
i. "I noticed that you were withdrawn today. Could you share with the group what's behind this?"

DISCUSSION SKILLS OBSERVATIONS

FEEDBACK ON SKILLS				COMMENTS
Nonverbal	H	M	L	
Questioning	H	M	L	
Empathy Feeling	H	M	L	
Genuine, clear Message —Feelings —Specific situation —Reasons	H	M	L	
Other	H	M	L	

Exercise 19.3

LEADING A DICUSSION GROUP

GOALS

In this exercise you will learn

1. to understand some basic concepts of discussion group facilitating, and

2. to practice leading a discussion group.

INTRODUCTION

Many leaders are called to facilitate a discussion group concerning an important topic. Often this skill is just putting together some of the skills learned earlier and used with a group of individuals.

DIRECTIONS

1. Read the information concerning *"Skills of the Group Discussion Leader."*

2. Discuss the information.

3. Form groups of five, one person playing the facilitator; one person, the observer.

4. Take one of the *"Sample Leadership Topics"* and discuss it for 15 minutes.

5. Have observer use the *"Observer Evaluation Form"* during the discussion and then provide feedback after the discussion.

6. Repeat the process until everyone has been both a discussion leader and an observer.

7. Review Exercise 19.1.

Exercise 19.3 (Continued)

SKILLS OF THE GROUP DISCUSSION LEADER

The building blocks of a good group leader are acceptance and listening.

When the facilitator is going to meet with the group, it is important to get them into a circle as quickly as possible. The circle can be on the floor or in chairs, but participants must be in a circle. Why a circle? Everyone has equal status; all of the members of a circle can see and communicate with all of the other members. Now that the circle has been established, the leader must understand that in any circle discussion two things should be occurring—acceptance and listening.

Acceptance

1. A process of accepting on the part of the leader the group members.

2. In the process of accepting, serious interaction needs to be taking place.

The facilitator needs to take as much as possible contributions with unconditional acceptance. This means developing the ability to accept honestly as worthwhile and valid every contribution that any member of the group makes. You must attempt to get over to the participants this acceptance of them that they are okay. You are expressing to them that you like them as individuals and accept them just as they are. In group procedure, when a facilitator has been able to develop this attitude of acceptance, the members will participate more freely and will discuss their genuine concerns.

Listening

As the facilitator, you will serve as the model. You will set the stage by listening carefully to both nonverbal and verbal methods by which to indicate to the members that you are listening. Some examples of nonverbal behavior are:

- The way you sit.
- Your facial expression.
- Your hand motions.

Your verbal methods can be

- Restating their questions.
- Reflecting on what they have said.
- Encouragement of the quiet members.

The verbal and nonverbal methods you utilize will indicate to the group members that you are listening. They will model after you, and also will begin to listen.

Organization

Let the group know the agenda by announcing ahead of time, giving them a written agenda, writing on the blackboard. Have the information needed for the group members ahead of time. Keep the group on task.

Exercise 19.3 (Continued)

Questions That Clarify

Ask questions that help the facilitator clarify in his/her own mind what the experience was or what the feeling was. Some examples of these types of questions are as follows:

1. What did you do when it happened?
2. Do you think that many people feel that way?
3. What do you think about that?
4. Do any of you have any questions that you would like to ask Joe?

QUESTIONING SKILLS

Open Invitations to Talk
(Open-Ended Questions)

An **open-ended question** encourages individuals to explore themselves and the concern held. Through the use of the open-ended question, the facilitator also communicates a willingness to assist the group members in the exploration. Open-ended questions help to

1. Begin a conversation.
2. Get the person to tell more about a point: "Could you tell me more about it?"
3. Facilitate the person understanding better: "What do you do when you get angry?"
4. Focus on the feelings of the person: "How do you feel about your assignment?"

A **closed question** often emphasizes factual content as opposed to feelings; it demonstrates a lack of interest in what individuals have to say and frequently keeps them in place. Closed questions can be answered by a few words or with a "Yes" or "No."

Basic Ways to Keep the Discussion Going

1. Raise pivotal questions.
2. Turn back questions to the group.
3. Allow silences for reflections.
4. Show acceptance by nodding, using positive words, or emphasizing key words.
5. Have the participants respond to each other rather than to the discussion leader.

SAMPLE LEADERSHIP TOPICS

1. The committee has $500 to spend in the next month. We need to decide by this meeting how it will be spent.

2. Discuss your feelings about the military draft.

3. Discuss ways to be supportive of someone trying to lose weight.

4. Discuss whether or not the proposed XYZ Committee should be allowed to form.

5. Assume that the group is a family, and discuss whether or not the offer to purchase a family home should be accepted.

6. Assume that you are the Publicity Committee within a local service club and are meeting to decide committee projects for the year.

Exercise 19.3 (Continued)

Name _____

Date _____ Hour _____

OBSERVATION EVALUATION FORM

Place a check mark under "High," "Medium," or "Low," designating how you rate the facilitator's skill level for each facilitator skill listed:

Skill	High	Medium	Low
Accepting	___	___	___
Listening	___	___	___
Questioning	___	___	___

In the same manner, rate the group members' response levels:

Response Level	High	Medium	Low
Trusting	___	___	___
Resistant or reluctant	___	___	___
Defensive	___	___	___
Responsive to other group members	___	___	___
Expressive of feelings	___	___	___
Expressive of thoughts (variety and depth)	___	___	___

Comments: _____

_____

_____

_____

_____

Exercise 19.4

LIFE PROBLEMS GROUP

GOALS

In this exercise you will learn

1. to give group members an opportunity to share with others the problems in their lives and to learn from others what problems they are experiencing, and

2. to provide a climate in which the group members may ventilate or work through their issues and share.

INTRODUCTION

Many successful groups are called "rap" groups; they focus on life's problems. This exercise will give you practice in facilitating and participating in a group relating to daily issues. Often no decisions are reached, except that some group members may themselves arrive at a decision for problems of their own. Others in the group may offer suggestions.

A list of sample statements is provided entitled "Let's Discuss" that may be used to provoke interest and lead to a discussion.

DIRECTIONS

1. Take the role that facilitates the group discussion.

2. Use almost exclusive attending and empathy skills with some questions.

3. Avoid giving facts or answering questions.

4. Avoid evaluation, judgment, interpretation, and probing questions.

5. Plan no agenda.

6. Use open-ended questions.

7. Divide the members into groups of five, with one being the observer.

8. Have one person be the facilitator, and change roles each time.

9. Use one or more of the topics entitled *"Let's Discuss,"* if your group does not start on their own.

10. Have the observer use the *"Group Feedback Form"* and after the discussion provide feedback.

11. Go back to Exercise 19.1 and evaluate yourself as a leader.

LET'S DISCUSS

Below is a set of sample statements that may provoke interest and lead to a discussion:

1. Academic problems are usually the result of students' disinterest in school and their putting more time and energy into complaining about a class than they do studying.

2. Academic problems seldom occur for students who are "B" or "A" students.

3. Good teachers usually don't have many students doing poorly. Bad teachers usually do.

4. Students should spend one to two hours a night doing homework.

5. When you study, your environment should be quiet and peaceful.

6. To do well in school, it is important to attend school regularly.

7. Usually a student can miss one day a week if they work very hard on the days that they are there.

8. In most classes it is not easy to know exactly how the teacher wants you to behave.

9. Teachers who have respect for students have more behavior problems with students than do teachers who appear tough and superior to the students.

Exercise 19.4 (Continued)

Name _____

Date _____ Hour _____

GROUP FEEDBACK FORM
(Facilitator Focus)

Name of Facilitator _____ Date _____

Name of Observer _____

Please check (X) the skills used by the facilitator during the activity, and place an (O) by the skills you would like to have seen him/her use.

____ Empathy	____ Attending
____ Clarifying	____ Ethical awareness
____ Summarizing	____ Techniques
____ Questioning	____ Modelers
____ Linking	____ Genuineness
____ Confronting	____ Group control
____ Blocking	____ Flexibility
____ Evaluating	____ Respect
____ Facilitating	____ Caring
____ Assertiveness	____ Problem solving

Comment on the exploration of the activity and the closure of the group.

_____

_____

_____

_____

_____

_____

Exercise 19.4 (Continued)

Other Comments: _____

_____

_____

_____

_____

_____

Exercise 19.5

SUBJECT MATTER GROUP

GOALS

In this exercise you will learn

1. to give the facilitator information in reference to the topic, and

2. to give the participants the opportunity to discuss issues.

INTRODUCTION

Many times you may want to discuss a particular subject with your group. To do so the facilitator needs to be familiar with the materials and to have ready what is needed. In subject matter discussions often no group decisions are made.

Individuals who understand and get along with others are sensitive to others' feelings. Therefore group members need to learn the effects of negative communication on both the giver and the receiver. This activity also gives the facilitator the opportunity to remind group members of how they mature in their ability to make good decisions. Make sure that no put downs occur in the group discussion.

DIRECTIONS

1. Divide into small groups of approximately five each with one member as leader of the discussion, one as observer, and others as discussants.

2. As a leader, facilitate the group and use basic listening skills, avoiding evaluation and agendas.

3. Have the leader of each group use one of the following topics:

  a. Discuss with the group as a whole:

   (1) What is a put down? How do you feel when you get put down?

   (2) What are some of the ways that we put individuals down (verbal, nonverbal)?

  b. Brainstorm these topics and list them:

   (1) Why do individuals give put downs (e.g., makes us feel important; we feel put down, they think they are just teasing)?

   (2) How do you feel after you have put someone down (guilty, ashamed, important)?

   (3) For what things do we get put down (these are often the same things that make us unique: tall, freckles, glasses)?

   (4) How can you handle put downs in a positive way (walk away; give yourself a put up; you don't have to believe it; tell them how it makes you feel)?

4. Have the observer use the *"Group Feedback Form"* during the discussion and as a basis for the feedback.

5. Have the observer to focus on discussants as well as observing the leader.

6. Write a short paragraph about a time that you felt put down. Include how it made you feel and what you did.

7. Have group members share their paragraphs; they should be allowed to "pass" if they wish. Each group chooses one of their situations to role play. Ask the group to brainstorm other ways that the put downs could have been handled. The group may want to do the role play again with a new ending.

8. Keep track of any put downs given or received for the next few days. Did the activity help to make them more sensitive?

9. Go back to Exercise 19.2, and check to see if the functions were followed.

Exercise 19.5 (Continued)

Name _____

Date _____ Hour _____

GROUP FEEDBACK FORM
(Member Focus)

Name: _____   Date: _____

Group Facilitator: _____   Group Activity: _____

Please give one copy to the group facilitator who in turn will give it to the instructor.

Please check the group members' reaction to the leader by indicating what you saw:

____   Trust   ____   Nonverbal behavior that you observed.

____   Resistance   ____   Game playing

____   Defensive behavior   ____   Listening to other members

____   A silent person   ____   Responding to other members

____   A monopolizer   ____   Express feelings

____   A sarcastic person   ____   Express thoughts

Please describe how the facilitator dealt with nonverbal behavior:

_____

_____

_____

_____

_____

_____

_____

Exercise 19.5 (Continued)

Other comments about the group members and how the facilitator handled the behavior of a specific group member:

_____

_____

_____

_____

_____

_____

_____

_____

Exercise 19.6

DECISION-MAKING GROUP

GOALS

In this exercise you will learn

1. to facilitate a problem-solving process, and

2. to assist the group in arriving at specific decisions that are acceptable to the group.

INTRODUCTION

Student groups, work groups, church groups are at times asked to make a decision about an issue. They often are called on to complete a task. This kind of group takes a great deal of skill for facilitators because they must keep the group members on task until they come to a decision.

ITEMS TO CONSIDER IN GROUPNESS

1. To what extent are the members compatible?

   a. Are the members friendly to each other?

   b. Do the members seem to like each other?

   c. Do the members seem to enjoy talking with each other?

   d. Do the members smile occasionally as they talk to the others?

   e. Do the members behave in ways that minimize the threat to others' egos?

2. To what extent does the group operate as a cohesive unit?

   a. Is there mutual helpfulness among the members?

   b. Do the members seem to be dependent on each other for support?

   c. Do the members seem eager to hear the group's reaction rather than proceeding on their own?

   d. Is there effort to bring deviates back to agreement with the group?

   e. Do the members seem more concerned with the group's interests than with self-interest?

   f. Do the members seem cooperative rather than competitive?

3. To what extent is the members' communicative interaction efficient?

   a. Which members contribute most; which, least?

   b. Which members' contributions are most helpful to the group?

   c. What kinds of information-opinion are contributed by each member?

   d. To which members are most communications directed?

   e. What proportion of communications is directed to the entire group?

   f. Are the members attentive listeners?

   g. Do contributions relate to and build on earlier contributions?

BRAINSTORMING

One technique that increases member participation and gets creative "juices" flowing is brainstorming. This technique will not necessarily generate better ideas, but it will promote "open-minded" and "divergent" thinking.

Four basic rules are to be followed when you use brainstorming, and it is important that you follow the rules if you want the technique to work:

1. Get the group members to think of at least one idea each—the more the better! Freely and quickly produce a list of the ideas. Keep the list visible at all times.

2. Criticism of an idea is **not allowed!** Group members should be told to defer judgment until later.

3. Free thinking and wild and crazy ideas are welcomed.

4. Combining two or more ideas is encouraged. This is done **after** the initial ideas are generated and represents a kind of synthesis, putting together of single ideas to form a unique or interesting combination.

Brainstorming consists of the following phases:

First phase (10-20 minutes). Introduce brainstorming topic. Spell out the ground rules, and proceed with actual brainstorming and listing of ideas.

Second phase (optional, 3-5 minutes). After a pause, set the group to work again and continue to list ideas. The best ideas frequently occur late in the session or during the "second round."

Third phase (5-7 minutes). Review the brainstorming list and clarify any confusion over ideas (e.g., "What did you mean by this?"). Also, connect similar ideas.

Exercise 19.6 (Continued)

Fourth phase (10 minutes). Ask the group to combine ideas that may fit together in interesting ways or to fit ideas into usable categories.

Approximate time allotments are given, but this can vary from group to group and from task to task.

DIRECTIONS

1. Use empathy to clarify ideas.

2. At times contribute your own ideas and feelings if needed to keep the group progressing.

3. Make sure the agenda is followed.

4. Appoint a recorder for your group who will keep record of the actions taken and discussions made.

5. Follow the steps for problem-solving (review the Problem-Solving Module).

6. Divide into groups of approximately five each with one person as the facilitator, one person as the observer, and the other three as the participants. The facilitator should follow the suggested format:

   a. Use one of the topics in the *"Suggested Decisions to be Made"* or one given by the instructor.

   b. State the issue (write on the board).

   c. Discuss all of the aspects of the issue.

   d. State the goal of the group.

   e. Brainstorm possible solutions (write on the board).

   f. Evaluate the solutions.

   g. Pick the best solution.

7. Have the observer to use items in the *"Observer Role"* and to provide feedback after the discussion.

8. Evaluate yourself using the material from Exercise 19.1.

Name _____

Date _____ Hour _____

SUGGESTED DECISIONS TO BE MADE

1. Your organization has just collected $1,000, and the task of the group is to decide how to spend the money.

2. Your church group has the opportunity to take a trip within 500 miles of the church to do missionary work. Help the group decide where they want to go.

3. Your work group is planning to purchase some new equipment. Your budget is $15,000. Please decide what is the best way to spend the money.

4. Other problems that you may want to solve.

OBSERVER ROLE

Did the facilitator:

	Yes	No
1. State the problem?	____	____
2. State the goal?	____	____
3. Help the group to clarify the issue?	____	____
4. Brainstorm the solutions?	____	____
5. Evaluate the solutions?	____	____
6. Pick the best solution?	____	____

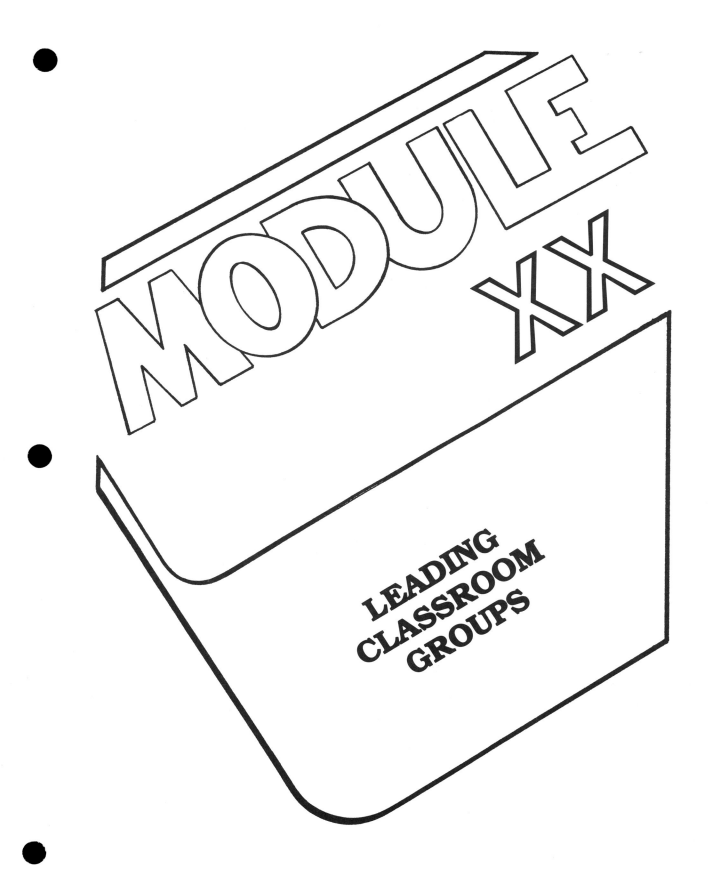

MODULE XX

LEADING CLASSROOM GROUPS

LEADING CLASSROOM GROUPS

As a peer helper, you may be called upon to lead large classroom groups on a variety of topics—health issues, value clarification issues, wellness, just say "No," and a variety of other topics. The skills needed for large classroom groups are somewhat different than one-on-one helping and small group discussion. Leading large classroom groups involves additional planning before the presentation, preparation of the material, motivation of the group for learning, and being aware of the different ways that persons learn. You also need skills in public speaking and being comfortable in front of large groups.

Your body language in front of a large group is very important. A variety of research studies indicates that 93% of the impact of a particular message depends on nonverbal cues. Another study indicates that 90% of the meaning that is transmitted between two individuals in face-to-face communication can come via nonverbal transmission. This has implications for a helper in large groups. Your posture and body language are very important and must be comfortable and consistent with the material that you are trying to present.

Another important piece of information is the fact that most individuals do not remember what is said. The normal, untrained listener is likely to understand and retain only about 50% of what is said and, 48 hours later, a mere 25%. As a leader of a large group, again, this has implications in that the audience needs to be motivated to listen. This can be achieved by such activities as having them involved in writing and/or talking about the topic. They need help in remembering what has been said. As a leader of a large group, provide activities for the audience so that they might write or discuss the information that is presented.

Use. This module should be taught after completion of *Peer Power: Book I* with its discussion skills module and exercises in tutoring. This module may be taught to high school, college, or adult groups. This is not designed to be a complete course in how to lead large groups.

Exercise 20.1

CHECKLIST OF SKILLS
FOR CLASSROOM GROUP

GOALS

In this exercise you will learn

1. to understand the different skills for classroom leading and other helping skills,

2. to check my own skill level, and

3. to be able to understand areas that need improvement.

INTRODUCTION

Different skills are needed for leading a classroom group, as compared to small discussion groups and one-on-one helping. You need to understand whether or not you have these skills and the differences among those skills.

DIRECTIONS

1. Look at the *"Skills of Helping"* chart to understand the differences among the different types of helping.

2. Look at the list of skills in the *"Skills Unique to a Large Classroom"* and check those that are your strengths, those possessed, and those on which you need assistance in developing.

3. Set a plan of action to improve those areas that need improvement. Spell out how you might obtain assistance from others in your group in helping you to develop one or more of the areas.

Name _____

Date _____ Hour _____

SKILLS OF HELPING

CODE: Some use = Y
Heavy Use = X

Skill	One-on-One	Small Group Discussion	Classroom
Attending	X	X	X
Empathy	X	X	Y
Summarization	X	X	Y
Genuineness	X	Y	Y
Assertiveness	Y	Y	Y
Confrontation	X	Y	Y
Problem Solving	X	X or Y*	Y
Planning	Y	X or Y*	X
Organizing	Y	X or Y*	X
Demonstrating	Y	Y	X
Monitoring	Y	X	X
Questioning	Y	X	Y
Evaluation	Y	Y	X
Public speaking skills			X

*Depends on the topic and type of group

SKILLS UNIQUE TO A LARGE CLASSROOM

Skill	Have as a Strength	Possess	Need Help to Develop
Attending			
Empathy			
Summarization			
Genuineness			
Assertiveness			
Confrontation			
Problem Solving			
Planning			
Organizing			
Demonstrating			
Monitoring			
Questioning			
Evaluation			
Public speaking skills			

Exercise 20.2

UNDERSTANDING OTHERS

GOALS

In this exercise you will learn

1. to understand how you learn best in a large group,

2. to understand the different ways that others learn, and

3. to develop activities to fit the different styles of learning.

INTRODUCTION

As you lead a classroom group, you need to understand that many and probably most individuals learn differently than you do. In working with a large group, it is not important to assess each person but to provide opportunities for all of the styles of learning.

DIRECTIONS

1. Review quickly Module 18 on tutoring to gain a better understanding of learning styles.

2. Look at the list of *"Different Ways to Learn"* and complete the chart.

3. Discuss with your training group how they learn best.

4. Brainstorm possible ways of leading a group that would fit each learning style.

5. Assume you are going to lead a large group lesson on How to Cook Breakfast. Give activity examples of how you would do this to meet the different learning styles.

Name _____

Date _____ Hour _____

DIFFERENT WAYS TO LEARN

Way of Learning	Check Ways You Learn Best—Give Examples	Give Examples for Others
1. Visual		
2. Auditory		
3. Tactile		
4. Talking		
5. Thinking		
6. Understanding big picture		
7. Step-by-step		
8. Other ways List: _____		

Exercise 20.3

MOTIVATING OTHERS

GOALS

In this exercise you will learn

1. to understand ways to motivate yourself, and

2. to understand ways to motivate others.

INTRODUCTION

To get the attention of your audience so that they will want to learn new information is a difficult task. Volumes have been written about ways to motivate learning. This exercise will help you think of ways that have motivated you and ways to motivate others.

DIRECTIONS

1. Listen to the trainer lead you through a visualization exercise.

2. Think of ways that have gotten you excited about learning something new. Complete the *"Ways of Motivating"* sheet.

3. Brainstorm ways of motivating large groups.

4. Think of short motivating activities to get individuals in a large classroom excited about learning how to get along with their peers.

Name _____

Date _____ Hour _____

WAYS OF MOTIVATING

Activities that motivated me to learn:

Ideas for motivating others:

Examples:

Explain why it's important to learn.
Recognition of learning a task.
Activities that are fun.

Motivating activities I have seen used effectively in large groups:

Exercise 20.4

PUBLIC SPEAKING SKILLS

GOALS

In this exercise you will

1. learn the specific public speaking skills that are needed, and

2. practice public speaking skills.

INTRODUCTION

If you are going to be leading a large classroom group, you will need good public speaking skills. You also will need to be a little bit of a "ham" and enjoy being in front of people.

DIRECTIONS

1   Review the *"Public Speaking Skills"* that are needed.

2. Practice giving short talks in front of the mirror and look at your nonverbal behavior.

3. Give a five-minute talk on a topic about which you know a great deal (e.g., how to swim, how to type, etc.) Use notes if that will help.

4. Ask the audience to give you feedback relative to your public speaking skills. They could use the list of *"Public Speaking Skills"* and check those that were done by you during your talk.

Exercise 20.4 (Continued)

PUBLIC SPEAKING SKILLS

1. Nonverbal

    a. Looked at audience

    b. Looked comfortable

    c. Gestures consistent with verbal content

    d. Good posture

    e. Looked balanced

    f. Other

2. Verbal

    a. Pleasant tone of voice

    b. Adequate volume

    c. Effective rate of speech

    d. Good clarity

3. Monitoring audience

    a. Kept audience's attention

    b. Focused on group

4. Organization*

    a. Introduction

    b. Presentation

    c. Conclusion

---

*Told them what I was going to say, said it, summarized what I said.

Exercise 20.5

Name _____

Date _____ Hour _____

PLANNING FOR LARGE GROUPS

GOALS

In this exercise you will

1. learn the steps in planning, and

2. learn to plan a lesson.

INTRODUCTION

Developing a plan of action for your large group is very important. The success of your lesson depends often on how organized you are.

DIRECTIONS

1. Examine the steps needed for planning a presentation.

2. Plan a lesson.

3. Work with the trainer for additional ideas.

4. Use the following lesson plan outline.

   a. Goals of the lesson

   b. Activities planned

   c. Materials needed

   d. Time needed for each activity

   e. Audio-visual aids needed

   f. Evaluation of learning

   g. Homework assignment

   h. Rules for classroom

5. Work in groups of three. Design a classroom presentation for 45 minutes on *"Good Listening Skills."*

6. Get help from the trainer.

Exercise 20.6

Name _____

Date _____ Hour _____

PRACTICE IN LARGE CLASSROOM GROUP PRESENTATION

GOALS

This activity will help you to

1. practice organizing a large classroom group,

2. practice leading a large classroom group, and

3. get feedback in reference to skills.

INTRODUCTION

Various topics can be presented to the classroom-size group. This is an opportunity to practice your skills in leading a large group.

DIRECTIONS

1. Study the two examples of classroom presentation:

   Classroom Exercise No. 1, Learning to Say "No"
   Classroom Exercise No. 2, Friendships

2. Select one of the two examples to present to your group.

3. Divide into groups of 4 or 5 members each.

4. Have enough materials for the group.

5. Select one member of your group to be the observer to give you feedback after leading the group.

6. Write on the board the goals of the presentation.

7. Write on the board the rules for the class.

   Examples:

   - Listen
   - Participate

8. Decide how long each activity should last.

9. Listen for feedback from the observer. Have the observer use the *"Observer Form."*

Exercise 20.6 (Continued)

OBSERVER FORM

Skills	Rated Good	Rated Adequate	Needs Improvement
The leader:			
1. Was organized	————	————	————
2. Had public speaking skills	————	————	————
3. Monitored the group	————	————	————
4. Motivated the group	————	————	————
5. Had communication skills	————	————	————
6. Demonstrated nonverbally	————	————	————
7. Was questioning	————	————	————
8. Facilitated discussion	————	————	————
9. Did homework	————	————	————
10. Other	————	————	————

Exercise 20.6 (Continued)

CLASSROOM EXERCISE #1

LEARNING TO SAY "NO"

GOAL

To learn how to say "No."

INTRODUCTION

Being able to say "No" is a characteristic that influences every area of one's life and is useful at many levels of interaction: teenagers being pressured by friends to use drugs, a boy or girl being pressured by a date to engage in sex, a student being pressured by friends to help them cheat on homework, and a person of any age being pressured on various sides to take on more and more responsibility to the point of overload. In our society, individuals need to know, first, that they have a right to say "No" and, second, that it is an assertive response that is very effective.

DIRECTIONS

1. Explain the above rationale to the group.

   a. You have the right to say NO.

   b. An aggressive way to do this is with a hostile attitude that really puts the other persons down and usually results in bad feelings on their part. Contrast aggressive with assertive responses.

   c. A passive response is to sound and look wishy-washy. This usually results in the other person's respecting your wishes. However, in the case of someone who persists, the recommended technique is to say "No," say "No" again, and finally walk away.

   d. An assertive response is a simple "No," said firmly and with an attitude of pride in yourself and respect for the other person. This usually results in the other person's respecting your wishes. However, in the case of someone who persists, the recommended technique is to say "No," say "No" again, and finally walk away.

2. Explain that the message that you convey is carried in more than just the words you say. It is also carried in your body language, tone of voice, and facial features.

3. Ask the class for an example of an aggressive response to a friend who wants to copy your homework. (Example: "No way, you jerk!" said with a loud, hostile voice and with aggressive body language.)

4. Ask the class for an example of a passive response to the same question. (Example: "Well, I. . .I don't know . . ." said with a voice trailing off faintly, eyes downcast, and slumping shoulders.)

Exercise 20.6 (Continued)

5. Ask the class for an example of an assertive response. (Example: "No, I don't do things that way," said with a firm voice, direct eye contact, and erect posture.)

6. Hand out activity sheet, Learning to say "No." Ask the class to complete this with assertive responses, individually or in pairs. Then ask them to pick items that they would like to discuss. Ask for volunteers to role play some of the more popular choices.

7. Hand out activity sheet, When I've Said "No." Ask the class to complete the worksheet. Explain that they will not be forced to share their responses, although this is encouraged. When they are finished writing, if the leader starts off with personal experiences, this will encourage the class to do likewise.

8. Ask the class to pair off to practice. One person should ask the other to do something that that person does not want to do. The other person just stands straight, looks the other person in the eye, and says "No." Then reverse the roles. It may help if the class were to agree on a standard situation to use. When everyone has had a turn in both roles, ask how they felt saying "No" and having "no" said to them. Probably the tendency is to want to explain when they say "No." Perhaps all will agree that they need to elaborate somewhat, even if only slightly.

9. The activity The Girl (or Boy) Who Couldn't Say "No" is optional.

10. Role playing is sometimes hard to get going. But if the leader can persuade two students to do the first one (or if the leader can be a part of the first one), the activity then usually flows very smoothly.

Name _____

Date _____ Hour _____

LEARNING TO SAY "NO"

Directions: How would you say "No" in the following situations? Write down what you would say. Try to say "No" so that the other person will not be angry, if possible.

1. You are a student who refuses to give a classmate the answers to the homework assignment due that day.

   _____

   _____

   _____

   _____

   _____

   _____

2. You are a person who says "No" to an offer to join in drinking or taking drugs.

   _____

   _____

   _____

   _____

   _____

   _____

3. You are a person with a lot of work to get done; you say "No" when friends ask you to go with them on a shopping trip.

   _____

   _____

   _____

   _____

   _____

WHEN I'VE SAID "NO"

Directions: Complete the following sentences. Be prepared to discuss your responses with the class.

1. The times I should have said "No," but didn't.

_____

_____

_____

_____

_____

_____

_____

_____

2. The times I said "No," and was glad I did.

_____

_____

_____

_____

_____

_____

_____

_____

_____

Exercise 20.6 (Continued)

Name _____

Date _____ Hour _____

THE GIRL (OR BOY) WHO COULDN'T SAY "NO"

Directions: Write a story about a boy or girl who couldn't say "No," and what happened to that person.

_____

_____

_____

_____

_____

_____

_____

_____

_____

_____

_____

_____

_____

_____

_____

_____

_____

_____

_____

_____

CLASSROOM EXERCISE #2

FRIENDSHIPS

GOAL

To understand what it takes to be a friend.

INTRODUCTION

Explain to the class that no one is perfect all the time. There is probably no one in the world who would not like to do a better job of making and keeping friends and establishing and maintaining meaningful relationships. We can all improve in these areas. We can learn to make new friends and get along better with those that we have.

DIRECTIONS

1. Introduce the participants to these words:

   Friendship
   Clique
   Condescending
   Relationship
   Authoritarian
   Combative
   Peer

2. Give each person a copy of the handout, *"Self-assessment of Friendship."*

3. Instruct the class to respond to each of the ten items on the handout.

4. After the class members have completed the handout, arrange them in ten small groups. Assign each group one of the ten items from the handout. Ask each group to list ways to improve on that item.

5. After completing the small group assignment, ask one person from each small group to read aloud the list compiled by that group.

6. Lead a group discussion regarding the responsibilities of friendship.

7. Encourage the students to brainstorm a long list (approximately 100) of relationships (write the list on the board), explaining that all relationships have rules.

8. Divide the class into pairs. Each pair may select one relationship from the brainstormed list and agree on four rules for that relationship. Tell the pairs to write down their four rules.

9. When the entire group has completed the assignment, select one person from each pair to identify the relationship by the pair and read their four rules aloud.

10. Lead a group discussion that centers around the following:

   a. A confidential relationship exists when two persons agree to share only with each other. Name some confidential relationships.

   b. Each relationship has a basis. Name a relationship that is based on money; on winning.

   c. Name two relationships that are disapproved of by society.

   d. In some cases a person pays another person to have a relationship. Name a paid relationship.

   e. What are some of the reasons for having difficulty finding and maintaining meaningful personal relationships?

   f. How do you define "meaningful personal relationship?"

   g. How do you determine whether or not you can trust another person in a relationship?

   h. Peer groups, commonly called cliques, seldom tolerate relationships outside the clique. Why is that?

   i. Write a relationship that is the most difficult for you to establish.

   j. Write a relationship that you are forced into by circumstances but would eventually like to break.

11. Give each student a copy of the handout, *"Relationships."*

12. Students may complete independently the handout. Do not expect the students to share their responses on this handout. It is too risky. This handout is meant to help the students become aware of the concept of analyzing and labeling relationships.

Name _____

Date _____ Hour _____

SELF-ASSESSMENT OF FRIENDSHIP

	Yes	No	Some-times
1. I am glad that something good happens to a friend, even though I wish it had happened to me.	——	——	——
2. I stick up for my friend.	——	——	——
3. I will give up doing something I want to do in order to help a friend.	——	——	——
4. When a friend tells me a secret, I don't tell anyone at all.	——	——	——
5. When I agree to do something for a friend, I try to keep my word.	——	——	——
6. In an argument, I try to see my friend's point of view, and I try not to get angry if they should disagree with me.	——	——	——
7. If I get angry and say something hurtful without thinking, I tell my friend later that I'm sorry.	——	——	——
8. I try to answer honestly when a friend asks for my opinion.	——	——	——
9. I try to be as courteous to my friends as I am to individual whom I don't know.	——	——	——
10. I try to do little things to please my friends.	——	——	——

Exercise 20.6 (Continued)

Name _____

Date _____ Hour _____

RELATIONSHIPS

Directions: From you own life, give one example of each of the following kinds of relationships:

Authoritarian _____

Combative _____

Condescending _____

Supportive _____

Helping _____

Dependent _____

Consulting _____

Destructive _____

Directive _____

Competitive _____

Serving _____

Loving _____

MODULE XXI

RECOGNIZING EATING DISORDER PROBLEMS

MODULE **21**

RECOGNIZING EATING DISORDER PROBLEMS

We all worry about food sometimes, overeat on holidays, and skip a meal. But individuals with eating disorders do more than worry; they live in constant fear of food and fat, often struggling to hide eating patterns that they cannot control.

Eating disorders are serious, addictive, progressive, and dangerous illnesses. They often result in physical effects, causing malnutrition, kidney failure, gastrointestinal damage, heart attack, or even death. In fact, up to 20% of those individuals with eating disorders die as a result of their illness and its effect.

Eating disorders are certainly not rare. Between 10% and 20% of young females suffer from bulimia or anorexia nervosa. A large number of individuals suffer from obesity.

Obesity, bulimia, and anorexia have become huge problems; and it is no wonder, in a culture that spends billions on diets, and where "this is in."

If you are concerned about an eating disorder in yourself, a friend, or family member, you don't need to feel alone or ashamed. Eating disorders are common and treatable. The first step to feeling good about yourself and food again is to

1. recognize the symptoms,
2. learn about eating disorders, and
3. plan for lifelong recovery.

WHO'S AT RISK?

Individuals try to hide an eating disorder, whether they binge, binge and purge, or starve. "Binging" means out-of-control eating—often thousands of calories at a time, quickly and without pleasure. Obesity, a medical problem can result from binging (also called compulsive overeating). Bulimics binge and then purge (getting rid of food, often vomiting or taking laxatives or other purging). Anorexics simply starve themselves.

While each eating disorder problem is different, all eating disorders share similar warning signs—an unhealthy amount of body fat and unusual thoughts, feelings, and behavior about food:

1. Body Fat. Too much or too little body fat is an obvious warning sign. You can measure when your body fat is dangerously high or low by using the *"Body Mass Index (BMI) Chart."* Draw a line from your weight (left column) to your height (right column). Is your BMI (see following Index) in the healthy range?

BODY MASS INDEX (BMI) CHART

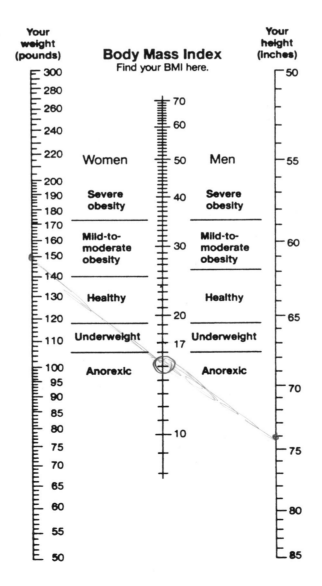

2. Constant dieting on low-calorie, high-restriction diets.

3. Using body weight and lack of fat to measure your own and others' worth.

4. Seeing your body image much differently than others see you.

5. Constantly talking and thinking about food (or refusing to talk about it).

6. Using food to cover up feelings such as loneliness, anger, or other negative feelings.

7. Exercising obsessively (more than 3 times a week for 30 minutes of vigorous exercise), unless you are in training for a sport.

8. Fear of not being able to stop eating once you start.

9. At times feeling food drunk.

10. Abusing alcohol or other drugs before binging.

11. Sometimes avoiding social situations involving food.

12. Oversensitivity to criticism, perfectionism.

13. Wearing bulky clothes to hide thinness.

14. Unusually strong concerns over school performance.

15. Low self-esteem.

SYMPTOMS AND PROBLEMS ASSOCIATED WITH EACH EATING DISORDER

Anorexia Nervosa

Anorexia is a compulsive, obsessive, addictive disease that can lead to malnutrition, starvation, permanent organ damage, and death if not treated and arrested. Of the individuals with anorexia nervosa, 97% are white and female. It hits 1 out of every 250 adolescent girls. They are generally high achievers in school and come from a very dependent family (family depends on them at an early age). Often a great deal of anger is present toward the family during illness.

Warning signs

1. Refusal to maintain body weight:

   —Loss leading to maintenance of body weight 15% below expected.

   —Failure to make expected gain during period of growth leading to body weight 15% below expected.

2. Intense fear of becoming obese even when underweight.

3. Disturbance in the way in which one's body weight, size, or shape is experienced.

4. Hyperactivity.

5. Amenorrhea (in females), or loss of menstruation.

6. Excessive constipation.

7. Depression.

8. Loss of hair (on the head).

9. Growth of fine body hair.

10. Extreme sensitivity to cold temperatures.

11. Low pulse rate.

12. Low body temperature.

13. Obsessive thinking about intake.

14. Distorted thinking.

15. Anxiety alleviated only by weight loss and fasting.

Bulimia

Bulimia is also an eating disorder and is characterized by the binge-purge syndrome, where laxatives or intentional vomiting are used to expel just consumed food. The binge behavior that precedes each purge usually involves the rapid ingestion of large amounts of food. Some of the physical problems are often difficulty in swallowing and retaining food, swollen and or infected salivary glands, damage to the esophagus sometimes causing pain and/or internal bleeding, bursting blood vessels in the eyes, excessive tooth decay, loss of tooth enamel, weakness, headaches, dizziness.

Symptoms

1. Recurrent episodes of binge eating.

2. During the eating binges, a feeling exists of lack of control over the eating behavior.

3. To prevent weight gain, the individual usually engages in

   - Self-induced vomiting
   - Use of laxatives
   - Fasting
   - Use of diuretics
   - Vigorous exercise

4. Frequent weight fluctuations.

5. Persistent overconcern with body shape and weight.

6. A minimum average of two binge-eating episodes per week for at least three months.

Bulimia is common among adolescents, and its prevalence is on the rise.

Obesity (Compulsive Overeaters)

The medical and social problems identified with obesity can be manifested in many ways. Obesity may decrease the lifespan, aggravate the onset of physical problems, and modify the social and economic quality of life. Obesity contributes to diabetes, heart problems, high blood pressure, pulmonary problems, digestive problems, and cancer. Social attitudes toward obesity range from cruelty toward children to economic discrimination against adults in employment. Many of these problems can be relieved with weight reduction.

Warning Signs

1. Body image distortion.

2. Binge on food.

3. Poor self-esteem.

4. Body weight more than 20% above the limit for height, excluding clothing.

5. Obese females having body fat at 30% body weight and the obese males having body fat at 25% of body weight.

Some of the factors that contribute to eating problems are the fact that many of these individuals are female and from the upper-middle socioeconomic class. Often a family type is present of either overweight or underweight. Sometimes physical abuse or sexual trauma is or has been present. Much has to do with sociocultural pressures that involve the hype on thinness and glamour. We also know that certain personality styles are more susceptible to eating problems.

Is this you?

Jim is a teenage boy who is full of energy and is very attractive. His day goes like this: he get eight hours of sleep and rises feeling refreshed. He wakes at 5:30 to shower for school and has plenty of time for breakfast with the family. A typical breakfast may include an egg, whole wheat toast, high-fiber cereal, orange juice, and milk. Jim maintains lots of energy through the morning and takes a gym class. For lunch, Jim eats a Type A lunch, which includes food from the four food groups and milk. After school, Jim has a snack of fruit and milk and then jogs for 30 minutes with his dad every other day. Later he goes to his part-time job and returns home about 6:30. Dinner is nutritious and comes from the four food groups. During homework time or time with his friends, he has a snack of fresh fruit and milk before going to bed.

If this is you, then you probably will not need to read this module for yourself. So read it to understand others.

Use. This module could be taught separately, or it could be placed early in training as awareness. It is appropriate for high school and older adults. The module is not designed to be a complete program in coping with eating disorders. Most individuals suffering from eating disorders need multiple interventions such as medical, nutritional, and psychological help. Often recovery is a long-term process.

A reference book for those who want to explore more about bulimia is Bauer, Anderson, and Hyatt's *Bulimia: Book for Therapist and Client*, Accelerated Development Inc., Muncie, Indiana.

Exercise 21.1

Name _____

Date _____ Hour _____

FOOD CHART

GOAL

This activity is designed to help you analyze your eating habits and to see some of what triggers poor eating habits.

DIRECTIONS

1. Review the information in the introductory material for Module 21.

2. Keep a *"Food Intake Log"* for the week.

3. Discuss with other peer helpers some of their eating habits.

4. Set some eating goals for yourself for the following week.

5. Discuss with the trainer the following:

    a. What did you learn from this activity?

    b. How are you going to change?

Date _____

FOOD INTAKE CHART

	Breakfast	Midmorning	Lunch	Afternoon	Before Dinner	Dinner	After Dinner
Time: Start	-	-	School lunch	snack	-	balanced meal	-
End							
Mood: Depressed							
Bored							
Happy							
Fatigued							
Excited							
Angry							
Other							
Foods and Amounts*							
Who prepared the food							
Eaten alone or with whom							
Exact place where eaten							
Activities while eating**							

*Small, medium, or large serving
**Reading, cooking, talking, etc.

Exercise 21.2

Name _____

Date _____ Hour _____

ASSESSING EATING DISORDERS

GOALS

In this exercise you will learn

1. to identify the potential for an eating problem, and

2. to learn some warning signs for self and others.

DIRECTIONS

1. Please respond to the questions in the *"Self-Assessment Check List on Eating Disorders."*

2. After reviewing the information in the introduction to Module 20 and completing the *"Self-Assessment Check List on Eating Disorders,"* write how you feel about your eating behavior.

3. Keep a journal during the next few days relative to your eating habits.

SELF-ASSESSMENT CHECK LIST ON EATING DISORDERS

Please check "Yes" or "No":

	Yes	**No**
1. Do you eat lots of food in a very short time?	✓	
2. Do you try to lose or maintain your weight by:		
Self-induced vomiting?		✓
Use of laxative?		✓
Diuretics?		✓
Diet pills?		✓
Excessive exercise?		✓
3. Do you binge or hide food?		✓
4. Has the amount of money (too much or too little) you spend on food become a problem in your life?		✓
5. Do you crave certain foods such as sugar, starch, or fattening foods?		✓
6. Has a family member threatened you because of your eating habits or tried to bribe you to change your habits?		✓
7. Is your overuse of food destroying your feelings of self-worth?		✓
8. When you change your food intake, do you experience depression, irritability, sleep disturbance, headaches, or feelings of weakness?		✓
9. Do you continue to eat late in the evening or early in the morning?	✓	
10. Do you feel that your eating problems are caused by problems in other parts of your life?		✓
11. Do you eat large amounts of food as a way of dealing with stress?		✓
12. Have you started diets in the last three months?		✓
13. Have you forced yourself to go on rigid diets or fasts?		✓
14. Do you minimize your eating problems with others?		✓

Exercise 21.2 (Continued)

Name _____

Date _____ Hour _____

	Yes	**No**
15. Are your family, employer, or friends concerned about your eating problems?	✓	
16. Do you frequently eat more than you intend?		✓
17. Do you feel guilty about your eating habits?		✓
18. Does your weight fluctuate because of overeating or undereating?		✓
19. Are you concerned because your eating is not normal?		✓
20. Are you a perfectionist?	✓	

If you have answered Yes to three or more, you may need to see a professional.

REACTIONS TO MY EATING BEHAVIOR

I do not believe that I have an eating disorder just because of this survey. I tend to not eat a lot of food in the morning and then eat an about normal dinner. My mom worries that I'm not eating right but it doesn't bother me

Exercise 21.3

Name _____

Date _____ Hour _____

BULIMIA, ANOREXIA, COMPULSIVE OVEREATING: WHERE ARE YOU AS AN EATING DISORDER PERSON OR ENABLER?

GOALS

In this exercise you will learn

1. how far you are in terms of the addiction of an eating disorder, and

2. how far you are in terms of enabling another with an eating disorder.

DIRECTIONS

1. Please study the two charts—*"Progression of Symptoms of Anorexia-Nervosa and Bulimia,"* and *"Compulsive Overeating Chart."*

2. Identify where you are in terms of eating problems.

3. Complete the *"Co-dependent Personality Check List"*

4. Review the check list and deduct where you are in enabling another person with an eating disorder.

5. Complete the following two statements:

   a. The stage I am in as a person with an eating disorder is

   I have a slight undereating problem, but nothing really serious. I tend to not eat all day and then have one big meal.

   b. The stage I am in as a co-dependent to someone with an eating disorder is

   I don't feel that I am a co-dependent to someone with an eating disorder

PROGRESSION OF SYMPTOMS OF ANOREXIA-NERVOSA AND BULIMIA

Anorexia	Bulimia

Beginning Symptoms

Low self-esteem	Low self-esteem
Misconception of hunger	I'm O.K. = low body weight
Feel out of control with life	I need others' approval
Distorted body image	Normal weight
	Always worry about weight

Help Needed

Over achiever	Try purging (vomiting, laxatives, diuretics)
Menstrual cycle stops	Fear of binge eating
Preoccupation with eating	Embarrassment
Isolates from family and friends	Depression
Compulsive exercising	Eats alone
Fights with family and friends	Gastrointestinal difficulty
Tries to control family eating	Anemia
Fatigue	
Increased facial and body hair (lanugo)	
Dishonest/Lying	

Critical Symptoms
(Should seek intensive professional help)

Thin dry scalp	Tooth decay
15-25% Loss of body weight (looks emaciated)	Binging
Feelings of control over body	Drug and alcohol abuse
Rigid	Laxative and diuretic abuse
Depression	Mood swings
Fear of gaining weight	Sore throat
Malnutrition	Difficulty swallowing
Mood Swings	Low potassium
Inability to think	Electrolyte imbalance
Denial of problems	Physical problems
Joint pain	Rupture of heart or esophagus
Sleep disturbance	Irregular heart rhythms
	Suicidal tendencies

Name _____

Date _____ Hour _____

Individual Cry for Help

Intervention

Acceptance of Problem either Anorexia-Nervosa or Bulimia

Appropriate Weight
Learn to Relax
Normal Eating Patterns
Involved With People
Diminished Fears
Return of Regular Menstrual Cycle
Acceptance of Personal Limitations
Acceptance of Spiritual Values
More Understanding of Family
Increased Optimism
Improved Self-Image
Increased Assertiveness
Honesty
Comfortable with World
Know Personal Needs
Intimacy—Trust and Openness

Ongoing Support

Family and Friends and some Professional Support

COMPULSIVE OVEREATING CHART

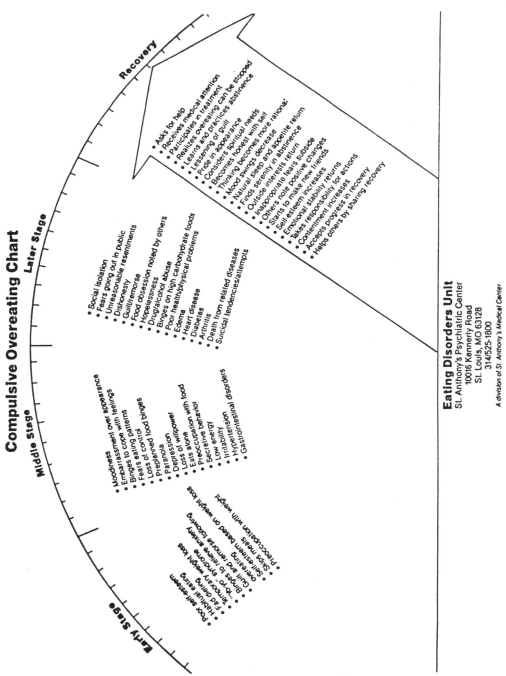

Compulsive Overeating Chart

Recovery
- Asks for help
- Receives medical attention
- Participates in treatment
- Realizes overeating can be stopped
- Learns and practices abstinence
- Lessening of guilt
- Pride in appearance
- Considers spiritual needs
- Becomes honest with self
- Thinking becomes more rational
- Mood swings decrease
- Natural sleep and appetite return
- Finds serenity in abstinence
- Outside interests return
- Inappropriate fears subside
- Others note positive return
- Starts to make new friends
- Self-esteem increases
- Emotional stability returns
- Takes responsibility for actions
- Contentment increases in recovery
- Accepts progress in recovery
- Helps others by sharing recovery

Later Stage
- Social isolation
- Fears going out in public
- Unreasonable resentments
- Dishonesty
- Guilt/remorse
- Food obsession noted by others
- Hopelessness
- Drug/alcohol abuse
- Binges on high carbohydrate foods
- Poor health/physical problems
- Edema
- Heart disease
- Diabetes
- Arthritis
- Death from related diseases
- Suicidal tendencies/attempts

Middle Stage
- Moodiness
- Embarrassment over appearance
- Binges eating patterns
- Fears to cope with feelings
- Fears of control
- Loss of control food binges
- Preplanned
- Paranoia
- Depression
- Loss of willpower
- Eats alone
- Eats occupation with food
- Preoccupation behavior
- Secretive
- Low energy
- Irritability
- Hypertension disorders
- Gastrointestinal disorders

Early Stage
- Poor self-esteem
- Habitual dieting
- Fad dieting
- Temporary weight loss
- "Yo-yo" syndrome
- Guilt and remorse following
- Skips meals
- Self-esteem based on weight loss
- Overeating
- Binges to relieve anxiety
- Preoccupation with weight loss

Eating Disorders Unit
St. Anthony's Psychiatric Center
10016 Kennerly Road
St. Louis, MO 63128
314/525-1800
A division of St. Anthony's Medical Center

Used by permission.

Name _____

Date _____ Hour _____

CO-DEPENDENT PERSONALITY CHECK LIST

Check the ones that apply:

Early Co-dependency

_____ 1. Grew up in a dysfunctional family and learned to take care of others in order to feel good about myself.

_____ 2. Failed to help parents so will help eating disorder person.

_____ 3. Tries to find eating disorder persons so as to control them.

_____ 4. Wants to control the eating of others so as to show decisiveness.

_____ 5. Is not involved with others socially because of always needing to help others.

Middle Co-dependency

_____ 6. Makes pleas and threats related to the eating problem.

_____ 7. Judges self and feels the cause of eating behavior.

_____ 8. Hides food.

_____ 9. Attempts to control eating by hiding food, making idle threats, nagging, scolding.

_____ 10. Shows anger and disappointment regarding eating disorder promises.

Advanced Co-dependency

_____ 11. Becomes obsessed with watching and covering up.

_____ 12. Takes over responsibility of eating disorder.

_____ 13. Takes a pivotal role in communications excluding contact between eating disorder person and others.

_____ 14. Expresses anger inappropriately.

Out of Control

_____ 15. Makes violent attempts to control eating. Fight with eating disorder.

_____ 16. Lets self go physically and mentally.

_____ 17. Obsessed with outside interest—work, drinking, other affairs.

_____ 18. Becomes rigid, appears angry most of the time.

_____ 19. Many have related illness and drug abuse: ulcers, rashes, migraines, depression.

_____ 20. Constantly loses temper.

_____ 21. Feels tired and ill most of the time.

SCORING

1-3 checked: Continue to be with that person and make contact.

4-7 checked: Push the person to obtain professional help.

7+ checked: Take action and inform a professional mental health worker about this person and try to get additional help.

Exercise 21.4

FOOD CHOICE EVALUATION

GOAL

This activity will help you discover if you are using foods that are in the four food groups.

DIRECTIONS

1. Complete the sheet entitled *"Food Record"* over a three-day period.

2. Refer to the *"Food Choice Evaluation"* sheet and follow the procedures.

3. Review *"Dietary Goals Applied to Four Food Groups."*

4. Review the *"Food Selection Changes"* sheet and your *"Food Record."* In so doing make changes in your *"Food Record"* that would have improved it.

5. Analyze your eating behavior to identify patterns, if any.

6. Establish eating goals for yourself.

FOOD CHOICE EVALUATION

1. Take one copy of summary entitled *"Dietary Goals Applied to Four Food Groups."*

2. Using the right column marked "Use Carefully," circle any food item from that column that appears on your *"Food Record."*

3. Scoring tips:

    a. Draw a circle for every portion consumed:

        Example: 3 cups coffee with sugar = 3 circles
                       2 beers = 2 circles
                       4 caffeinated sodas = 4 circles

    b. Draw a circle for each "Use Carefully" component in a combination food:

        Example: Sausage and cheese pizza = 2 circles
                       (a processed meat)

4. Scoring key:

Number of Circles per Day		Rating
11 or more	=	Disaster diet
8 to 10	=	Danger zone
5 to 7	=	Doing better
4 or less	=	Clean living

Name _____

Date _____ Hour _____

FOOD RECORD

Name _____David Young_____

Date	Kind and Quantity Food	Date	Kind and Quantity Food	Date	Kind and Quantity Food
1/23/92		1/24/92		1/25/92	
Time		**Time**		**Time**	
Physical activity		**Physical activity**		**Physical activity**	

DIETARY GOALS APPLIED TO
FOUR FOOD GROUPS

Food Group	Choose Daily	Use Carefully!
Milk	Lowfat and nonfat milks Cottage cheese Lowfat yogurt	*Whole and chocolate milks *Cheddar-type cheeses *Processed cheeses *Ice cream
Meat	Lean meats Fish, poultry Dry beans & peas Soy extenders	*High fat & organ meats *Eggs, shrimp *Salted nuts *Salted & processed meats
Fruit & Vegetable	Most fruits & vegetables	*Vegetables with sauce *Avocados *Fruits packed in syrup

Bread & Cereal	Whole grain breads
	Whole grain or enriched
	  cereals without excess
	  sugar
	Rice, noodles, pasta
		Sweet baked goods
		*High sugar cereals; check
		  "natural" cereals too
		*Salted crackers

Other	Vegetable oils	Sweetened beverages Alcoholic beverages Salty snack chips Candy Honey, sugar, jelly, syrup Salty condiments *Canned soups Butter, meat fats

*These foods contribute significant amounts of nutrients.

Name _____

Date _____ Hour _____

FOOD SELECTION CHANGES

As suggested by *U.S. Dietary Goals,* published by the Senate Select Committee on Nutrition and Human Needs, Second Edition, 1977.

1. To avoid being overweight consume only as much energy (calories) as is expended; if overweight, decrease energy intake and increase energy output.

2. Increase intake of fruits, vegetables, and whole grains.

3. Decrease intake of refined and other processed sugars and foods high in such sugars.

4. Decrease intake of foods high in total fat; partially replace saturated fats, whether obtained from animal or vegetable sources, with polyunsaturated fats.

5. Decrease intake of animal fat; choose meats, poultry, and fish, which will lower saturated fat intake.

6. Except for young children, substitute low-fat and nonfat milk for whole milk and low-fat dairy products for high-fat dairy products.

7. Decrease intake of butter, eggs, and other high cholesterol sources (may need to ease the cholesterol goal for premenopausal women, young children and the elderly in order to obtain nutritional benefits of eggs in the diet).

8. Decrease intake of salt and foods high in salt content.

Name _____

Date _____ Hour _____

CULTURAL IMPACT ON EATING DISORDERS

GOALS

In this exercise you will learn

1. to examine the cultural aspect of eating disorders, and

2. to get in touch with how you see yourself in the culture as far as an eating disorder person.

DIRECTIONS

1. Obtain several popular magazines to review and to cut apart.

2. Look in the magazines for pictures of individuals—are they representative of the general population?

3. Notice the amount of emphasis placed on diet and beauty in the magazines.

4. From the magazines make a collage representing yourself.

   - Cut out pictures and words that describe how you see yourself.

   - Glue materials on posterboard.

5. Discuss the pictures with the group.

   - Explain how the collage represents you.

   - How much emphasis is on beauty, body size, and so forth?

6. React to your collage; do you want to be different?

7. Turn in an essay at the next training meeting concerning the impact of the culture on eating disorders.

Name _____

Date _____ Hour _____

PRACTICE IN HELPING A PERSON
WITH AN EATING DISORDER

GOAL

This activity will help you as a peer helper

1. to practice confronting a person with an eating disorder, and

2. to role play working with a person with a possible eating disorder.

DIRECTIONS

1. Divide into triads.

2. Have one person to play the role of someone who has an eating disorder. The following are examples of roles:

   a. Sue has been eating very little in the last six months. Every time she eats a half of cup of yogurt, she thinks she is eating too much. She spends a very small amount of money on food, and she thinks continually that she is too fat, especially in her stomach. She is very thin.

   b. Jim is at least 75 pounds overweight, seems very depressed, and eats junk food nonstop. It is normal to see him eat at least a dozen donuts every time he has breakfast. He always carries junk food with him.

3. Have one person to play the helper (use empathy, questioning, and confrontation skills).

4. Have one person to be an observer and coach. Use the
   "Guide for the Observer."

5. Change roles so that each person in the group has a chance to practice.

6. Discuss with the entire training group the following:

   a. What intervention techniques were used?

   b. How did it feel playing the role of the helper?

   c. How did it feel role playing the part of the person with an eating disorder?

   d. Did the helper ask questions concerning eating disorder issues?

7. Prepare a list of local resources and professionals for referral sources regarding eating disorders. Use the *"Referral Resources"* sheet and add to it.

Exercise 21.6 (Continued)

GUIDE FOR THE OBSERVER

	High	Medium	Low
1. Use of attending	____	____	____
2. Use of empathy	____	____	____
3. Use of confrontation techniques	____	____	____
4. Use of getting additional help	____	____	____
5. Ability to assess eating disorder person	____	____	____

	Open	Closed
6. Use of questions	____	____

	Yes	No
7. Did a good job of being supportive	____	____

Exercise 21.6 (Continued)

Name _____

Date _____ Hour _____

REFERRAL RESOURCES

List local hospitals that offer help for eating disorders to either inpatient or outpatient.

Referral sources of professional counselors who can be referred to for proper medical, dietary, or psychological intervention.

National Resources

AMERICAN ASSOCIATION OF EATING DISORDERS COUNSELORS
2324 South Cost Highway
Laguna Beach, California 92651

714-494-8227

ANOREXIA, BULIMIA INC.
Post Office Box 213
Lincoln Center, Massachusetts 01773

ANOREXIA NERVOSA AND RELATED EATING DISORDERS
Post Office Box 5102
Eugene, Oregon 97405

AMERICAN ANOREXIA/BULIMIA ASSOCIATION
133 Cedar Lane
Teaneck, New Jersey 07666

201-836-1800

THE BRIDGE/NATIONAL ANOREXIC AID SOCIETY
4897 Karl Road
Columbus, Ohio 43229

W.E.L.L. PROGRAM
(Well-Eating for Life: A program for anorexia,
    bulimia, and compulsive overeating)
Sponsored by Rohen and Associates
    and St. Joseph Hospital
Behavioral Medicine
ST.JOSEPH HEALTH CENTER
300 Capitol Drive
St. Charles, Missouri 63301

314-947-5311 or 800-835-1212

Exercise 21.6 (Continued)

NATIONAL ASSOCIATION OF ANOREXIA NERVOSA
AND ASSOCIATED DISORDERS
Post Office Box 271
Highland Park, Illinois 60035

312-831-3438

BASH
1035 Bellevue Avenue, Suite 104
St. Louis, Missouri 63117

ANOREXIA NERVOSA AID SOCIETY
OF MASSACHUSETTS, INC.
Box 213
Lincoln Center, Massachusetts 01773

617-259-9767

Exercise 21.7

Name _____

Date _____ Hour _____

LOOKING AT MYSELF

GOALS

This activity will help you

1. to review the learning from Module 21, and

2. to set goals for changing behavior.

DIRECTIONS

1. Please discuss with your group and the trainer the following:

   a. How much is my self-esteem associated with my body image?

      Now

      Future goal

   b. How much do I use food to deal with stress?

      Now

      Future goal

   c. How much are my thought patterns distorted about my eating behavior?

      Now

      Future goal

   d. How do I use food as a replacement for being close with people?

      Now

      Future goal

2. Use *"My Goal for the Future"* to identify personal goals. Discuss these with the trainer.

MY GOAL FOR THE FUTURE

My goal for the future is to do the following:

1.

2.

3.

4.

_____
Participant signature

_____
Trainer signature

MODULE XXII

SUICIDE PREVENTION

MODULE **22**

SUICIDE PREVENTION

Suicide has been the epidemic of the 80s and is projected to continue in the 90s. Many newspaper articles talk about the fact that adolescent suicide is on the rise. During the past five years adolescent suicide has moved from being the third leading cause of death among 11-year-olds to 24-year-olds to the second leading cause. Only accidents rank higher. Some even believe that many accidents are actually suicides.

Why has suicide become epidemic? Many of today's adolescents think of suicide as being an acceptable option in dealing with stress. What has been found is that one suicide often triggers multiple attempts and some completions. Many adolescents who have attempted suicide have come from a family where a previous suicide or an attempted suicide has occurred. An interesting note is that, by the time a child graduates from high school, the typical child has seen 17,000 violent television deaths and rock videos depicting aggression. The Committee on Youth Suicide recently announced that one of every ten teens will make a bonafide attempt by the age of 19 years. Every 90 minutes someone in the United States between the ages of 15 and 25 years commits suicide. This adds up to 5,800 American lives wasted each year.

The adult population is not much better in that the National Center for Health Statistics indicates that suicide is the eighth leading cause of death. For the population of 65 years and older it is the thirteenth leading cause of death. The bottom line is that every 24 minutes someone dies by his or her own hand.

Boys typically are four times more likely to commit suicide than are girls, although as our society changes, girls become more susceptible to suicide. In fact suicides affect every age, race, color, and socioeconomic part of our society.

According to the Youth Suicide National Center, the following factors have a direct bearing on the level of risk of teenage suicide:

- Family history of suicide or suicidal behavior

- Previous suicide attempts

- Recent suicide of a friend or relative

- Withdrawal from family and/or friends

- Expressing suicidal thoughts or threats

- Major personality changes

- Changes in eating or sleeping habits, appearance, energy level, or interest in friends or activities

- Outbursts of violent or rebellious behavior

- Running away

- Trouble with the law, friends, authorities

- Difficulty concentrating

- Drug and/or alcohol abuse

- Unexplained decline in the quality of schoolwork or athletics

- Feeling "different" from family or friends

- Rejection by boyfriend or girlfriend

- Lack of confidence in the future

- Giving away cherished possessions

As you know, the time of adolescence is one of the most stressful times in one's life. It is often a very turbulent time. Suicidal adolescents may experience feelings of loss, helplessness, hopelessness, loneliness, and isolation. These feelings may be attributed to stressful events that often occur during adolescence for example, events such as getting married, unwed pregnancy, death of a parent, acquiring a visible deformity, divorce of parents, fathering an unwed pregnancy, and becoming involved in drugs and alcohol. More general events that contribute to stress with teenagers are loss of self-esteem; breakdown of the family unit through separation, divorce, or death; frequent moves and transferring to new schools; break up of a romance; concern over homosexual feelings; pressure to achieve in school; peer pressure to belong to a social group; and suicidal death of a friend or family member.

Barry D. Garfinkel, Director of the Division of Child and Adolescent Psychiatry, University of Minnesota Medical School, cautions that three general areas must be examined in attempting to identify potential suicide victims:

1. incidence of depression in the youth population,

2. various psychosocial stresses affecting the students, and

3. their methods of responding to and handling difficult problems.

Much of the research on suicidal behavior and depression indicates that a majority of the reported subjects who are depressed are suicidal or have suicidal thoughts. The important thing is that not all depressed individuals are suicidal and not all suicide victims are depressed.

Some of the psychosocial stressors affecting the adolescent are simply the adolescent experience. This might include problems with sexual development, low self-esteem, poor communication, high achievers with low self-esteem, poor problem-solving skills, and lack of resources for help. Also high stress may exist among family members. Families may not be open to communication; various situations may not be dealt with by the family such as moves, deaths, dual-career families, single parenting.

Specifically, if you have a friend who exhibits one or more of the following signs, you may want to help that friend to get professional help:

- Themes of death and dying in the person's writing and artwork

- Abusive use of drugs and/or alcohol

- Making final arrangements (saying good bye, giving away prized possessions)

- Loss of an important person or thing

- Sudden happiness or energy following a depression

- Depression

- Previous suicide attempts

- Talking or threatening to kill or harm oneself

Several signs at one time would tell you for certain that the person needs help.

A variety of facts and myths surround suicide. Following are just a few:

Myth: People who talk about suicide never do it.
Fact: The individual who talks about it does commit suicide; therefore, listen to what the person is saying.

Myth: Suicide happens without warning.
Fact: There is generally some warning such as feeling sad or taking a few pills.

Myth: Suicide victims come only from lower class families.
Fact: Suicide crosses all socioeconomic groups and no one class is more susceptible to it than another.

Myth: Once an adolescent is suicidal, that adolescent is suicidal for-ever.
Fact: Most adolescents are suicidal for a limited time—for 24 to 75 hours around a crisis.

Myth: The adolescent who attempts suicide and survives will never make another attempt.

Fact: Counseling is needed for this adolescent or each attempt will get worse.

Myth: Most adolescents who commit suicide leave notes.

Fact: Only a small percentage leave notes.

Myth: Every adolescent who attempts suicide is depressed.

Fact: This is true of many, but some just want to leave a situation, while some even seem happy because they have decided to "resolve" all of their problems at the same time.

Myth: The correlation between alcoholism and suicide is very low.

Fact: Alcohol, drugs, and suicide often go hand in hand.

Myth: The tendency toward suicide is inherited.

Fact: It is not in the genes; however, individuals often share an emotional climate that uses suicide to manage stress—low level of self-esteem—and suicide becomes an appropriate way of coping.

Myth: If you ask a person about his/her suicidal intention, you will encourage that person to kill himself/herself.

Fact: Actually, the opposite is true. Asking someone directly about suicidal intent will often lower the anxiety level and act as a deterrent to suicidal behavior by encouraging the ventilation of pent-up emotions.

Myth: Because of the holiday season, December has a high suicide rate.

Fact: There is a low risk of suicides at Christmas, and December has the lowest suicide rate of any month.

Use. This module could be taught separately, or it could be used by the peer helper in advanced training for use in helping individuals, small group discussions, or large group presentations. This is not meant to be a complete guide to suicide prevention. It is appropriate for middle school and above. For more complete work, please read Howard Rosenthal's *Not With My Life I Don't* and Dave Capuzzi and Larry Golden's *Preventing Adolescent Suicide*, both published by Accelerated Development Inc., Muncie, Indiana.

Exercise 22.1

Name _____

Date _____ Hour _____

HOW STRESSFUL ARE YOU?

GOALS

In this exercise you will learn

1. to understand your own stress level, and

2. when to get additional help is appropriate.

DIRECTIONS

1. Review the material from the introduction to Module 22.

2. Take *"The Teen Scene: Stress Test."*

3. With the trainer's leadership, discuss the items and possibly your scores on the stress test.

4. Brainstorm techniques for reducing stress.

5. Start a journal on your feelings and reactions to the exercises and group work relating to suicide.

6. Outline a plan based on your stress test results to deal with your stress.

7. Develop goals related to dealing with stress in your life.

Exercise 22.1 (Continued)

THE TEEN SCENE: STRESS TEST

	Often	Some-times	Seldom	Never
1. During the past three months have you been under considerable strain, stress, or pressure?	✓			
2. Have you experienced any of the following symptoms: palpitations or a racing heart, dizziness, blushing, painfully cold hands or feet, shallow or fast breathing, nail biting, restless body or legs, butterflies in stomach, insomnia, chronic fatigue?			✓	
3. In general, do you have headaches or digestive upsets?		✓		
4. Do you have any crying spells or feel like crying?				✓
5. Do you have any recurring nightmares?				✓
6. Do you experience pain in your neck, back, or arms?			✓	
7. Do you feel depressed or unhappy?			✓	
8. Do you worry excessively?		✓		
9. Do you ever feel anxious even though you don't know why?				✓
10. Are you ever edgy or inpatient with your parents or other family members?		✓		
11. Are you ever overwhelmed by hopeless-ness?				✓
12. Do you dwell on things you should have done but didn't?			✓	
13. Do you dwell on things you did but shouldn't have?			✓	
14. Do you have problems focusing on your schoolwork?			✓	

Exercise 22.1 (Continued)

Name _____

Date _____ Hour _____

	Often	Some-times	Seldom	Never
15. When you are criticized, do you brood about it?			✓	
16. Do you worry about what others think?			✓	
17. Are you bored?		✓		
18. Do you feel envy or resentment that someone has something you don't?				✓
19. Do you quarrel with your boy/girlfriend?				✓
20. Are there serious conflicts between your parents?			✓	

	Yes	No
21. Lately do you find yourself more irritable and argumentative than usual?		✓
22. Are you as popular with your friends as you'd wish?	✓	
23. Are you doing as well in school as you'd like to?	✓	
24. Do you feel that you can live up to your parents' expectations?	✓	
25. Do you feel that your parents understand your problems and are supportive?		✓
26. On the whole, are you satisfied with the way you look?	✓	
27. Do you have trouble with any of your teachers?		✓
28. Do you sometimes worry that your friends might be turning against you?		✓
29. Do you have enough spending money to cover your needs?	✓	
30. Have you noticed lately that you eat, drink, or smoke more than you really should?		✓
31. Do you make strong demands on yourself?	✓	
32. Do you feel that the limits imposed by your parents regarding what you may or may not do are justified?		✓
33. Do your parents always criticize you?		✓

	Yes	No
34. Do you have any serious worries concerning your love relationships with the opposite sex?		✓
35. Are any of your brothers or sisters overly competitive with you?	✓	
36. Do you feel left out in social gatherings?		✓
37. Do you habitually fall behind in your school work?		✓
38. Do you feel tense and defensive when you're around someone your age of the opposite sex?		✓
39. Have you, or has anyone in your family, suffered a severe illness or injury within the last year?	✓	
40. Do you experience any conflict between peer pressure to engage in certain activities and your own standards?		✓
41. Have you recently moved to a new home, school, or community?		✓
42. Have you been rejected by a boy/girlfriend within the last three months?		✓
43. Is it very difficult for you to say "no" to requests?	✓	
44. Have your school grades taken a sudden drop lately?		✓
45. Do you often become ill after an emotional upset?		✓

Name _____ David Luverg _____

Date _____ Hour _____

Scoring

Add up your points for the Stress Test results based on this answer key:

		(ST)	(S)	(N)			Yes	No
1.	(O) ⑦	4	1	0	21.		4	⓪
2.	7	4	①	0	22.		⓪	3
3.	6	③	1	0	23.		⓪	4
4.	5	2	1	⓪	24.		⓪	6
5.	6	3	1	⓪	25.		0	⑤
6.	4	2	⓪	0	26.		⓪	4
7.	7	3	①	0	27.		3	⓪
8.	6	③	1	0	28.		4	⓪
9.	6	3	1	⓪	29.		⓪	3
10.	5	②	0	0	30.		5	⓪
11.	7	3	1	⓪	31.		④	0
12.	4	2	⓪	0	32.		0	③
13.	4	2	⓪	0	33.		4	⓪
14.	4	2	0	⓪	34.		5	⓪
15.	4	2	⓪	0	35.		③	0
16.	4	2	⓪	0	36.		4	⓪
17.	4	②	0	0	37.		3	⓪
18.	4	②	0	⓪	38.		3	⓪
19.	5	3	1	⓪	39.		⑥	0
20.	5	3	①	0	40.		5	⓪
					41.		3	⓪
					42.		4	⓪
					43.		③	0
					44.		4	⓪
					45.		5	⓪

44

Exercise 22.1 (Continued)

Results

116-203 Troubles outnumber satisfactions, subject to high level of stress

- Avoid stressful situations and get in control of your life.

- Learn effective ways to manage stress.

- Get professional help.

65-115 Moderate level of stress

- You're handling frustration well.

- You have occasional difficulties handling stress.

0-61 Low stress level

NOTE: Teen Scene Stress Survey by Dr. Eugene Roundsepp was published in *Harper's Bazaar*, July 1985, used by permission.

Exercise 22.2

Name _____

Date _____ Hour _____

SUICIDE RISKS

GOALS

In this exercise you will learn

1. to understand others who are at risk for suicide, and

2. to understand your own level of suicide risk.

DIRECTIONS

1. Read the categories in the *"Suicide Risks Test"* and check the ones that apply to you or to someone whom you are helping.

2. If you check more than three, talk to the person whom you are trying to help into seeing a professional counselor.

3. Review the suicide risk factors as listed in the *"Suicide Risks Test"* and discuss these with other participants.

4. Work in small groups to develop intervention strategies for reducing risk factors.

5. Continue to write in your journal.

6. Plan an intervention plan to obtain professional help for someone with several risk factors.

Exercise 22.2 (Continued)

SUICIDE RISKS TEST

Directions: Check those items that apply.

_____ 1. Talking or threatening to kill or harm oneself.

_____ 2. Previous suicide attempts.

✓ 3. Severe depression (feelings of hopelessness, helplessness, loneliness, withdrawal, and changes in appetite, sleep and school or work performance—this is sometimes seen in people with sleep disorders, anorexia, or weight loss).

_____ 4. Sudden energy following a depression (energy is needed to commit suicide).

_____ 5. Loss of an important person or thing, ideal, or self-esteem.

✓ 6. Making final arrangements (saying good bye, getting rid of friends, giving away prized possessions).

_____ 7. Abusive use of drugs and alcohol.

_____ 8. Themes of death and dying in the person's writing and artwork.

✓ 9. High stress in the person's life (see 22.2) or, if the person is an adult, look at loss of loved ones by death, divorce or separation; loss of job, money, prestige; sickness; changes in life or environment.

✓ 10. The person seems to have a suicide plan that is logical and well thought out.

_____ 11. The person does not have many sources of support (does not have friends or family, or they are not available to help).

_____ 12. Severe health problems or constant complaints of illness.

_____ 13. Communication very limited; and, if tried to communicate, was not successful.

Results

1-3 checked*: Continue to be with that person and make contact.

4-7 checked: Push the person to get professional help.

7+ checked: Take action and inform a professional mental health worker about this person and try to get additional help.

*Discuss with your supervisor the behavior about which you are concerned.

Exercise 22.3

Name _____

Date _____ Hour _____

INTERVENTION TECHNIQUES

GOALS

In this exercise, it is important to have guidelines in talking to a potential suicide victim. The following are guidelines:

In this exercise you will

1. gain an understanding of what to do and what not to do in an action plan for the suicidal person, and

2. develop a guide for trying to help the suicidal person.

DIRECTIONS

1. Review and discuss things *"To Do as Suicide Intervention Techniques."*

2. Review and discuss *"Don'ts When Helping Suicidal Persons."*

3. Brainstorm with the entire group a plan of action in dealing with the potentially suicidal person.

4. Complete the sheet on *"My Options for Working With a Suicidal Person."*

5. Identify *"Other Intervention Techniques I Could Use."*

6. Develop a resource list of professional people and materials for use with suicidal persons and/or those affected by a suicide. Add to the *"Referral Resources"* list.

7. Continue your journal.

TO DO AS SUICIDE INTERVENTION TECHNIQUES

1. **Listen to the person, show support and interest.**

   - Listen for verbal cues and warnings such as "I can't go on." "I'm going to kill myself." "I wish I were dead." "Life has no meaning for me." "I'm getting out, I'm tired."

2. Listen to the degree of seriousness of the individual.

   - Does the person have a plan? Ask specifically whether or not that person has a plan to kill or harm himself or herself. The more detailed the plan, the greater is the risk.

3. Check out the thinking of the person. Does the person want

   - To join a friend or family member who has died?

   - To gain the attention of others?

   - To escape from a situation (poor homelife, no job, failure at school, no friends)?

   - To punish someone who has hurt him or her?

4. Take seriously any threats.

   - Do not try to humor the individual who talks about suicide; above all, do not laugh at that person.

   - Do not dismiss or undervalue what the individual is saying. In some instances, youths may express the difficulty in a low key, but beneath the seeming calm there may be profoundly distressed feelings. Take any suicidal talk seriously.

5. Remove all lethal weapons such as guns, pills, and razors.

6. Evaluate the resources available.

   - See if the person has the support of family or friends.

7. Ask for assistance and outside help.

   - Get professional help. Encourage the person to seek outside help from a counselor or other mental health practitioner who can help solve problems. If the person resists, you may have to get the help for them.

   - If the professional feels hospitalization is what is needed, support this approach and help the person deal with it.

8. Get others involved.

   - Arrange for a receptive person to stay with the person in the crisis (generally 24-75 hours).

   - Make the environment as safe as possible.

   - Offer and supply emotional support for reasons for living.

   - Give reassurance that depressed feelings are temporary and will pass.

9. Trust your instincts if you suspect that someone is suicidal.

Name _____

Date _____ Hour _____

DON'TS WHEN HELPING SUICIDAL PERSONS

1. Don't promise the suicidal person that you will swear to secrecy. You may lose a friendship, but you may save a life.

2. Don't argue with a suicidal person. That person may not realize that he has everything in the world to live for. Arguments may make the person more guilty.

3. Don't leave the person alone should you believe that the risk for suicide is immediate.

4. Don't try to handle the person alone. Get others involved (mental health professionals, police family).

5. Don't act shocked or be judgmental about what you have been told.

Exercise 22.3 (Continued)

MY OPTIONS FOR WORKING WITH A SUICIDAL PERSON

1. listen to the person show support and interest

2. degree of seriousness

3. Check out thinking of person what they want

OTHER INTERVENTION TECHNIQUES I COULD USE

1. outside help

2. make sure someone is with person at all times

3. family support

268   *Peer Power: Book 2*

REFERRAL RESOURCES

"Adolescent Suicide Prevention Programs:
A Guide for Schools and Communities,"
published by:
FAIRFAX COUNTY SCHOOLS
Belle Willard Ad Center
10210 Lazton Hall Center
Fairfax, VA 22030

AMERICAN ASSOCIATION OF SUICIDOLOGY
2459 South Ash Street
Denver, CO 80222
(303) 692-0985

NATIONAL COMMITTEE ON YOUTH SUICIDE PREVENTION
666 Fifth Avenue, 13th Floor
New York, NY 10103
(212) 247-6910

LIFE CRISIS SERVICES, INC.
1423 South Big Bend Boulevard
St. Louis, MO 63117
(314) 647-3100

NATIONAL SUICIDE HELP CENTER
Box 711
Clear Lake, IA 50428
(515) 357-HELP

Peer Facilitator Quarterly
EDUCATIONAL MEDIA CORPORATION
Box 21311
Minneapolis, MN 55421

Suicide Prevention: A Resource and Planning Guide
Publications Sales Office
WISCONSIN DEPARTMENT OF PUBLIC INSTRUCTION
125 South Webster Street
P.O. Box 7641
Madison, WI 53707

YOUTH SUICIDE NATIONAL CENTER
1825 I Street, N.W., Suite 400
Washington, D.C. 20006
(202) 429-2016

NATIONAL COMMITTEE FOR YOUTH SUICIDE PREVENTION
1811 Trousdale Drive
Burlingame, CA 94010
(415) 877-5604

SUICIDE PREVENTION CENTER, INC.
184 Salem Avenue
Dayton, OH 45406

SURVIVORS OF SUICIDE QUARTERLY
Suicide Prevention Center
184 Salem Avenue Dayton, OH 45406
First issue free, $8.00 per year

Grief After Suicide, pamphlet
Mental Health Association
414 West Moreland Boulevard, Room 101
Waukesha, WI 53186

Exercise 22.4

ASSISTING THOSE LEFT TO LIVE ON AFTER A SUICIDE

GOALS

In this exercise, you will learn

1. techniques for helping the survivors of suicide, and

2. to understand the impact on others of suicide.

INTRODUCTION

A successful suicide has a tremendous impact on the survivors. It seriously affects at least six to ten people on a long-term basis. It has a tremendous impact on entire communities, schools, and worksites. Professionals and peer helpers are needed to assist survivors of a suicide.

1. Assist others to cope with loss

   - Listen to them talk about the person that committed suicide.

   - You may be listening for a long time.

   - Help the person understand the *"Stages of Loss."*

2. Suggest that the persons join a survivor counseling group for family members and friends of the victim. Or they may want to meet individually with someone. Let them know that this may be long term.

3. Hundreds of individuals, if not entire communities, may need short-term help such as small group discussions; they need information about the dynamics of suicide.

4. Tell them that you are there to listen. Often just talking is very helpful, and you can be a help by serving in that role. Accept their happiness and sadness.

DIRECTIONS

1. Review *"Stages of Loss"* and typical statements made during these stages.

2. To gain a feel for this aspect of peer helping, assume you were a close friend of someone who committed suicide and write a short paragraph on how you would feel.

3. Write how you might react and/or feel to helping a survivor of suicide.

4. Outline a plan for assisting someone who is a friend of a person who committed suicide.

5. Brainstorm with other peer helpers about helping survivors.

6. Continue to write in your journal.

STAGES OF LOSS

Denial

"It isn't true!"

Anger

"How dare he pull a thing like that?"

Guilt

"Why didn't I realize this was going to happen?"
"I didn't do enough."

Sadness

"It's okay to cry. Don't hold it in for other's convenience."

Bargaining

"If I'd been more understanding, he might still be here."

Acceptance

"He had no other choice. I must go on with my life."

Exercise 22.5

PRACTICE IN HELPING A SUICIDAL PERSON

GOALS

In this exercise you will

1. role play working with a suicidal person, and

2. gain a better understanding for assisting a suicidal person to obtain assistance, professional and supportive.

DIRECTIONS

1. Divide into groups of threes.

2. Role play in the group a situation of someone considering suicide. (This person has just lost a best friend through suicide and has become very depressed, is not talking with the family, and recently slashed his wrist, which he has been hiding from others.) (Alternative: Listen to someone that has lost a best friend to suicide.)

3. Have one person play the helper and use attending, empathy, questioning, and confrontation skills in getting the person to professional help.

4. Have one person be an observer and provide feedback using *"Guide for the Observer."*

5. Change roles so that each person in the group has a chance to practice all three roles.

6. Discuss with the whole training group the following:

   a. What intervention techniques were used?

   b. How did it feel playing the role of helper?

   c. How did it feel to role play the part of the suicidal person?

   d. Did the helper ask questions concerning suicidal thoughts and action plans?

7. Record in your journal your feelings about this activity and submit your journal to the trainer.

Exercise 22.5

GUIDE FOR THE OBSERVER

Use of Skill	Circle			Comments
Attending	High	Medium	Low	
Empathy	High	Medium	Low	
Questioning	Open	Closed		
Confrontation	High	Medium	Low	

Use of Intervention Techniques

      Asking questions

      Getting additional help

Ability to Assess Suicidal Risk:

      Did a good job of asking questions

      Did a good job of being supportive

MODULE XXIII

COPING WITH LOSS

MODULE **23**

COPING WITH LOSS

Life is full of transitions and loss. Individuals and families cope differently with transitions and loss. The most difficult loss with which to deal is often death. Loss is also experienced in terms of moving from one place to another, losing a friendship, or loss of parent through divorce. At times, individuals experience loss through injury or illness. These times can be stressful and painful. If someone is willing to share the pain and the stress with the individual, it makes that time easier. Sometimes coping with loss takes years. Some individuals often go to professional counselors or a support group. As a peer helper you can perform an important role by assisting family and friends as they deal with loss. As a peer helper another important aspect is dealing with your own loss.

Use. This module can be used in advanced training to assist peer helpers to become aware of their own losses and also to assist others. It could be used at any age. This module could be used along with the module on suicide.

Exercise 23.1

Name _____

Date _____ Hour _____

MY OWN LOSSES

GOAL

To learn more about losses in my life.

INTRODUCTION

We all experience loss during our lifetime. This exercise will give you an opportunity to share some of those losses with others.

DIRECTIONS

1. Review the *"Age-Loss Line"* presented. Greater depth of the line means a greater amount of pain that resulted because of the loss.

2. Draw *"My Age-Loss Line."*

3. **Discuss within small groups or with the total group the Age-Loss Lines developed in Direction 2 and offer support to one another.**

4. Explore the coping that occurred at different losses.

5. Examine differences in feelings and coping when the losses were close together compared to greater time span between.

6. Record your reactions to the exercise.

Do

AGE-LOSS LINE

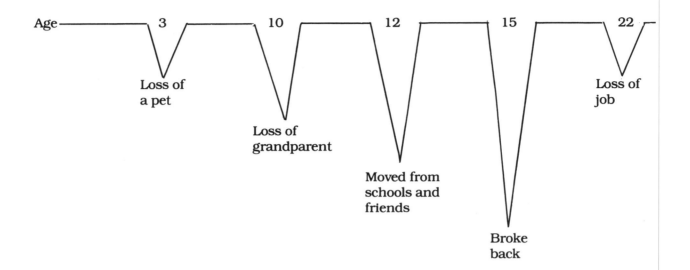

Age ——— 3 ——— 10 ——— 12 ——— 15 ——— 22

Loss of
a pet

Loss of
grandparent

Moved from
schools and
friends

Broke
back

Loss of
job

MY AGE-LOSS LINE

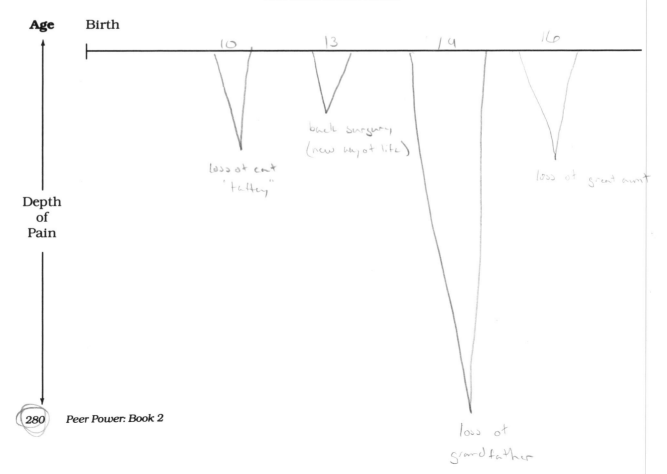

Age   Birth

10   13   14   16

Depth
of
Pain

loss of cat
"fatty"

back surgery
(new way of life)

loss of great aunt

loss of
grandfather

Exercise 23.2

Read

TYPES OF LOSS

GOALS

In this exercise you will learn

1. to get in touch with different types of losses,

2. to discuss coping mechanisms, and

3. to discuss the part that rituals play in coping.

DIRECTIONS

1. Review Column 1 in the *"Types of Losses."*

2. Add to Column 1 additional losses.

3. In Column 2 record how you coped with each of the losses that you have experienced.

4. In Column 3 record the ritual that helped, if any. Was the ritual formal and/or informal?

5. List ways you have learned in coping with loss.

6. Identify ways you can help others cope with loss.

7. Write your reaction to this exercise with a focus on coping with loss.

Exercise 23.2 (Continued)

TYPES OF LOSSES

Loss	How You Coped	Ritual That Helped
Death	- remembered good times - helped my Grandmother as much as possible	- kept gifts (autographed baseball, his poems, etc.)
Illness	- took my medicine - ate plenty of food	- 3 doses 2 times a day
Loss of friend	- kept in touch by phone and writing	- talk to as much as possible
Moving	- too young to remember	nothing
Divorce	N/A	nothing
Injury	- rested - rehabilitated myself	- friends visiting - grand mother stayed with me the whole time
Change school/work	- rejoiced because old job was hell	
Other		

Exercise 23.3

Real

THE GRIEVING PROCESS

GOALS

In this exercise you will

1. gain a better understanding of the grieving process, and

2. understand where you are in reference to grieving.

INTRODUCTION

To understand the grieving process is very important. This exercise addresses the process as presented by Kubler-Ross.

DIRECTIONS

1. Review and gain a better understanding of *"The Grieving Process."*

2. Explore your feelings in reference to grieving.

3. Discuss in the small or total group a loss that you have experienced and discuss where you are in the grieving process.

4. **Analyze what you gained from Directions 1, 2, and 3, and transfer your insights into how you can be helpful in working with others.**

5. Write your reaction to this exercise.

THE GRIEVING PROCESS

Webster's Dictionary explains grief as "a keen mental suffering or distress over affliction or loss." The loss of a loved one by death is not required to experience grief. Grief can be experienced in many ways: retirement, divorce, destruction of possessions through flood or fire, moving to a new location.

The following are stages in the grieving process and are listed in the order in which they generally occur.

- **Denial**—"It isn't true!"

  They deny that there is a problem.

Read

- **Anger**—"I'm so mad!"

  This stage asks "Why?" The concerned others become angry at themselves, at life. They let the loss control them and become lost in their own loss. The are consumed with self-pity.

- **Bargaining**—"Let's make a deal!"

  The thought process can be this: "I denied it, and it didn't go away. I raised the roof, and nothing happened.. Maybe I can make a deal." This is expressed by endless offers that start with, "If I had been better at helping, it shouldn't have happened."

- **Depression**—"There's nothing that can be done!"

  When anger does no good, when bargaining proves futile, they pass into depression.

- **Acceptance**—"Ok. That's the way it is, but I can change myself!"

  Remember, acceptance does not mean that you have to like it—just accept it!

NEGATIVE AND POSITIVE FEELINGS

Feelings in Grieving Process (Negatives)	**Feelings with Acceptance** (Positives)
Blaming	Understanding
Rage	Empathy
Bitterness	Sadness
Resentment	Disappointment
Envy	Pride
Insecurity	Security
Resignation	Hopeful
Lethargy	Action
Fear	Knowing
Isolation	Belonging
Frustration	Satisfaction
Guilt	Reorientation
Shame	Honor/Improved Self-Image

Exercise 23.4

Name _____

Date _____ Hour _____

OFFERING SUPPORT TO OTHERS

GOALS

In this exercise you will be able

1. to practice listening to someone who is dealing with loss, and

2. to offer referral possibilities.

INTRODUCTION

While individuals are going through the grieving process, you, as a peer helper, can be very helpful by being a friend and offering your support.

DIRECTIONS

1. Review *"The Grieving Process"* in Exercise 23.3.

2. Review referral possibilities. This may be the list developed in Exercise 22.3. In some communities you may be able to add to the list and/or substitute resources.

3. Divide into triads, with one person playing the role of the helper, one the role of someone who is coping with loss, and one the role of observer.

4. Have the observer give feedback to the helper concerning the basic skills using *"Guide for the Observer."*

5. Explore you feelings in the role of the helper, the helpee, and the observer.

6. Write your concepts about your role as support to someone experiencing grief.

Exercise 23.4 (Continued)

GUIDE FOR THE OBSERVER

	High	Medium	Low	Comments
1. Attending	——	——	——	
2. Empathy	——	——	——	
3. Genuineness	——	——	——	
4. Questioning	——	——	——	
5. Knowledge of grieving process	——	——	——	
6. Other points noted during the role-play	——	——	——	

MODULE XXIV

ETHICAL CONSIDERATIONS IN PEER COUNSELING/PEER HELPING

ETHICAL CONSIDERATIONS IN PEER COUNSELING/ PEER HELPING

When you are in the role of peer counselor/peer helper in training or actually helping others, issues related to ethics and conduct are important to understand. The terms peer counselor and peer helper are used interchangeably in this module. As you function as a peer helper, you need to realize that you are a role model for others and that a role model implies responsibilities. Since you are involved in training, significant issues around confidentiality need to be addressed. In peer helping, it is imperative that you operate ethically at all times. As part of your ongoing supervision you must discuss most of your activities with your trainer. As a program, certainly limits exist as to the kind of help that you can provide; therefore having access to local resources and national resources is helpful. A necessary step for any lay or professional helper is to develop a procedure for referrals.

Sometimes having a code of conduct developed for your peer counseling group is helpful not only for the peer counselors but also for the public receiving the service. Ethics are a guide of morals or values for peer counselors. A code of conduct is a guide to specific behaviors that are appropriate for the peer counselors in the local program.

As a peer counselor, an important procedure is to establish a network with other peer helpers. One good way to achieve this is to network with other programs in your area or state. You might do well to get involved with the National Peer Helpers Association. You may write to join and get copies of ethics statements by the national organization. The address of the NPHA is 2470 Market Street, Room 120, San Francisco, CA 94114.

Use. This module can be used at the very beginning of training and also as you start *Peer Power: Book 2.* A good idea is to review these thoughts throughout training and supervision.

Exercise 24.1

Name _____

Date _____ Hour _____

ETHICAL ISSUES IN TRAINING

GOALS

The goal is for you

1. to understand the ethical issues involved in training, and

2. to establish together with the other participants local norms for the peer helper/peer counseling group.

INTRODUCTION

Important procedures to understand are ethical issues involved in peer helping training and to develop local norms.

DIRECTIONS

1. Review the ethical *"Issues Important During Training."*

2. Use the sheet *"Local Norms"* to explore on your own expectations of yourself and of others in the training program.

3. Explore within the group and with the trainer local norms and consequences if broken.

4. As a group, develop local norms for the group. Have those duplicated and signed by each participant.

ISSUES IMPORTANT DURING TRAINING

1. **Confidentiality**

- Personal information learned during training is not to be shared with anyone else other than those involved in the training group.

- Trust is important for effective training.

- Trust is important for an effective peer counselor.

- Share activities and learning but not specific problems discussed by others.

- If you are aware of an adult trainer who breaks confidence, you need to discuss this with him or her.

Exercise 24.1 (Continued)

2. **Participation**

 - Trainees should participate in all activities.

 - Attendance is important.

 - **Trainees must be drug-free during training.**

 - Trainees should be able to learn to the fullest possible extent.

 - Trainees should be confident that other trainees are drug free during training.

3. The training should include adequate time to practice and master the skills.

4. The training should be adequate so that the peer counselor can perform the job.

LOCAL NORMS

Norm	Consequences if Broken
1. Confidentiality	I don't think that person needs to be kicked out but must be suspended and talked to.
2. Participation	Light punishment not too harsh
3. Drug free	Immediate removal from group
4.	
5.	

Exercise 24.2

Name _____

Date _____ Hour _____

CODE OF ETHICS FOR THE PEER COUNSELOR/HELPER

GOALS

You will learn

1. to understand a code of ethics when you are operating as a peer counselor, and

2. to develop a local code of ethics.

INTRODUCTION

When you are in the role of a peer counselor, it is important to have a local code of ethics.

DIRECTIONS

1. Write to the NPHA for Code of Ethics for the Peer Helper.

NATIONAL PEER HELPERS ASSOCIATION
2370 Market Street, Room 120
San Francisco, CA 94114

2. Review the material on *"Peer Counselor's Code of Ethics."*

3. Define each area from the *"Peer Counselor's Code of Ethics"* and apply it to your local situation.

4. Develop together with the trainer and other participants a written code of ethics and have it with you at all times.

Exercise 24.2 (Continued)

PEER COUNSELOR'S/HELPER'S CODE OF ETHICS

1. Confidentiality needs to be addressed.

2. Supervision needs to be outlined.

3. Limits of peer counselor. Issues to be referred to a professional mental health worker:

   - Suicide

   - Abuse

   - Pregnancy

   - Substance abuse

   - Illegal acts

   - Serious emotional problems

4. Conflict of interest. This implies that you not use the position of peer helper for personal gain.

5. Local program requirements should be followed.

6. Local code of conduct should be followed.

7. "Trust is the foundation for helping and being a good friend."

Exercise 24.3

Name _____

Date _____ Hour _____

KNOWING YOUR OWN LIMITS

GOALS

You will be able

1. to know possible referral sources, and

2. to know how to refer and when to refer.

INTRODUCTION

You must secure a list of local referral sources and what they do. The list is to be used as you work with individuals and groups. You will learn in this exercise how to refer helpees for professional help.

DIRECTIONS

1. Develop a list of *"Local Referral Sources"* using the outline provided.

2. Write for a list of local members of The National Professional Mental Health Workers.

3. Develop a procedure for giving referral sources to peer helpees.

4. As a peer counselor identify your limits and learn when you need to refer.

5. Identify how you would make a referral using *"Guidelines for Referral."*

6. Agree to follow the guidelines established by your Peer Counseling Program. Your trainer may ask you to sign such a statement.

Exercise 24.3 (Continued)

LOCAL REFERRAL SOURCES

LOCAL PROFESSIONALS

Develop a list of local referral sources:

Private psychologists

Private counselors

Private social workers

HOT LINE NUMBERS

- Drugs and alcohol

- AIDS

- Pregnancy

- Other

DROP-IN CENTERS

- Youth Crisis Centers

SUPPORT GROUPS

- NA

- AA

- Al-Anon

- OA

- Grieving groups

- Others

HOSPITALS

- Drug and alcohol programs

- Other

NATIONAL SOURCES

You may write to these organizations and get a list of their local members.

AMERICAN PSYCHIATRIC ASSOCIATION
1400 K Street N.W.
Washington, D.C. 20005

AMERICAN PSYCHOLOGICAL ASSOCIATION
1200 17th Street N.W.
Washington, D.C. 20006

NATIONAL BOARD OF CERTIFIED COUNSELORS
5599 Stevenson Avenue
Alexandria, VA 22304

AMERICAN ASSOCIATION FOR MARRIAGE
   AND FAMILY THERAPY
1717 K Street N.W., #407
Washington, D.C. 20006

GUIDELINES FOR REFERRAL

1. Discuss possible referral with the sponsor or peer counseling group.

2. Decide whether or not the helpees should meet with the sponsor first. Sit in on the meeting.

3. Help by giving your phone number to the helpees and volunteering to offer your support.

4. If you were not able to accompany the helpees, follow up to see if they went.

5. With any life threatening problems, go immediately to the sponsor or professional mental health person in your program.

Add additional guidelines.

Exercise 24.4

Name _____

Date _____ Hour _____

CODE OF CONDUCT

GOAL

You will be able

1. to develop a code of conduct for local peer counselors, and

2. to discuss the issues relative to a code of conduct.

INTRODUCTION

A local code of conduct is a personal guide for peer counselors. The code of conduct must fit the values of the peer counselor, program requirements, and local rules and laws.

DIRECTIONS

1. Discuss trust and its meaning.

2. Discuss role model and its meaning.

3. Identify state laws (e.g., child abuse) that will need to be understood as a peer helper.

4. Identify local regulations that will need to be understood as a peer helper.

5. Use the *"Code of Conduct Guidelines"* and develop *"Your Own Code of Conduct."*

6. Discuss with other peer helpers the items they identified in Directions 3 and 4.

7. Think through what you will do if your values conflict with the local program goals.

8. Identify what you will do if you disagree with the local rules.

CODE OF CONDUCT GUIDELINES

1. Local rules and regulations

2. State laws

3. Program behavior code

    Examples

    - Confidentiality

    - Drug free

    - Knowing limits

    - Participation

    - Other

YOUR OWN CODE OF CONDUCT

_____

Peer Counselor

_____

Trainer

Exercise 24.5

Name _____

Date _____ Hour _____

DEALING WITH ETHICAL ISSUES

GOALS

In this exercise you will learn

1. how to deal with ethical issues,

2. how to refer back to program standards and ethical issues developed locally and nationally, and

3. to put into practice the code of conduct.

INTRODUCTION

By discussing possible situations that you may encounter, you may become aware of ethical violations.

DIRECTIONS

1. Review the *"Examples of Unethical Situations"* and identify how the code of ethics or code of behavior has been violated.

2. Discuss the consequences of behavior indicated in the *"Examples."*

3. Give some of your own examples and relate each to the code of ethics or code of behavior.

4. Discuss in the group those other examples identified by other peer helpers.

EXAMPLES OF UNETHICAL SITUATIONS

1. A peer helper, who is going through training on problem solving, has helped another trainee solve a problem about that trainee's family. The peer helper talks to the peer helper's mother about the problem and has identified who the trainee is.

2. The trainee has been smoking pot every day before coming to training.

3. The peer helper has been using the peer helper's position to get friends out of class.

4. The peer helper has been making fun of a person whom the peer helper is tutoring to another peer helper and the tutee hears the comments.

5. The peer helper without consultation or utilization of community resources has been trying to help a friend who is considering suicide.

6. The peer helper has been giving out phone numbers of abortion clinics in the area.

7. The peer helper is not prepared for the classroom presentation.

8. The peer helper does not have the skills to lead a small discussion group.

9. The peer helper skips class.

10. The peer helper breaks the code of conduct.

11. Other possible situations.

Exercise 24.6

Name _____

Date _____ Hour _____

NETWORKING

GOAL

To develop a plan of networking.

INTRODUCTION

In your role as a peer counselor, a meaningful procedure is to talk with others in the same role. Networking provides an opportunity to do this.

DIRECTIONS

1. Obtain information on the National Peer Helpers Association.

2. Develop a plan to meet regularly after completion of training with your own peer counseling group.

3. Identify a local support person with whom you can and will network.

4. Develop *"A Plan to Expand Your Local Networking"* with other peer counselors.

5. Develop a plan for *"Networking With Other Peer Helper Groups."*

A PLAN TO EXPAND YOUR LOCAL NETWORKING

LOCAL

1. Now

2. Expanded

NETWORKING WITH OTHER PEER HELPER GROUPS

1. Now

2. Expanded

    a. How to do this:

        • Workshop

        • Sharing meeting

        • Writing letter

2. Plan of action

    a. Who

    b. When

    c. Where

    d. How

3. What else is needed?

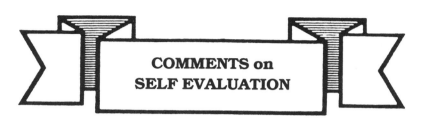

**COMMENTS on
SELF EVALUATION**

To the Peer Counselor/Peer Helper:

Please spend time to mark the self evaluation form after you have completed your training. You need to be aware of your skills, the range of your activities, the extent to which you have developed peer counselor qualities, and an indication of how you are performing in keeping with accepted peer counselor guidelines. This evaluation activity may be repeated from time to time as you function in your new role. You may want to share this self-evaluation with your supervisor.

Many professional people will be watching as you function as a peer counselor. Therefore you need to know your limitations as you act as a peer counselor. You also need to be extremely clear about your role so you can perform in a self assured manner.

Hopefully you will find helping others interesting, rewarding, and exciting enough to consider formal training in the human relations area. The field is extremely rewarding and constantly changing.

**SELF EVALUATION
for the
PEER HELPER**

PROGRAM OPERATION

Circle one for each item.

	Always	Often	Seldom	Never
1. I have a professional supervisor	A	O	S	N
2. I meet weekly with my supervisor	A	O	S	N
3. I contact my supervisor for assistance regarding individual problems of others whom I am helping	A	O	S	N
4. I refer people with more difficult problems to a professional counselor	A	O	S	N
5. I see my role as supplementary to the professional counselor	A	O	S	N
6. I have approval to function as a peer counselor from officials in the organization, agency, school, business, or industry of which I am a member	A	O	S	N
7. I am aware of the institution/school/agency guidelines for operation of a Peer Counseling Program	A	O	S	N
8. I see my role as a part of a larger program	A	O	S	N
9. I provide peer counseling activities in a designated place	A	O	S	N
10. I function at the level of my competency	A	O	S	N
11. I maintain records and share them with my supervisor	A	O	S	N

DIRECT HELPING RELATIONSHIP

	Always	Often	Seldom	Never
12. I secure information from the person I am helping by means of a structured interview	A	O	S	N
13. I provide information prepared in advance and approved by the professional supervisor for the people with whom I work	A	O	S	N
14. I provide information and support to former peers with whom I have worked	A	O	S	N
15. I perform outreach activities obtaining professional help for people	A	O	S	N
16. I can explain the peer counseling program to others	A	O	S	N
17. I participate in groups as a leader, co-leader, or active participant with the approval of my supervisor	A	O	S	N
18. I serve as a liasion between clients and professional counselor	A	O	S	N
19. I decide in consultation with my professional supervisor appropriate referral sources	A	O	S	N
20. I try to put others at ease and establish the beginning of a helping relationship that may be provided by me or a professional counselor	A	O	S	N

DIRECT HELPING RELATIONSHIP WITH GROUPS

	Always	Often	Seldom	Never
21. I guide discussions as a leader in a structured group with established program objectives	A	O	S	N
22. I provide material and information to the structured group in consultation with my supervisor	A	O	S	N
23. I observe verbal and nonverbal interaction in structured groups, and I follow good procedures for doing so	A	O	S	N
24. I participate in informal conversations in a small group of people with whom I might help	A	O	S	N

INDIRECT HELPING RELATIONSHIP

	Always	Often	Seldom	Never
25. I try to find new sources of information for the people I am trying to help	A	O	S	N
26. I obtain from my supervisor material for dissimination for educational, occupational, and personal-social information	A	O	S	N
27. I can operate a computer based career information system	A	O	S	N
28. I can dissiminate information regarding the agency/institution/school	A	O	S	N
29. I help develop written material about the Peer Counseling Program	A	O	S	N
30. I assist, as a proctor, in group testing	A	O	S	N

ROLE AS A PEER COUNSELOR/HELPER

	Always	Often	Seldom	Never
31. I function on a one-on-one counseling model	A	O	S	N
What kind of issues?				
32. I provide group leadership	A	O	S	N
What kind of groups?				
33. I provide help to others through career search	A	O	S	N
34. I provide tutoring	A	O	S	N
35. I work with people new to the agency/institution/school	A	O	S	N
36. I work with persons other than my peers	A	O	S	N
37. I can assist a professional counselor in an intervention activity	A	O	S	N

PREPARATION OF THE PEER HELPER

	Always	Often	Seldom	Never
38. I have met the criteria set up by my agency/institution/school for a peer counselor	A	O	S	N
39. I understand my role as a peer counselor	A	O	S	N
40. I have completed the total available Peer Counselor Training Program	A	O	S	N
41. As a peer counselor, I feel comfortable working with the population I serve	A	O	S	N
42. I have the technical skills to perform the tasks assigned to me	A	O	S	N

43. I have integrated the following skills into my helping relationships:

	Always	Often	Seldom	Never
a. attending	A	O	S	N
b. empathy	A	O	S	N
c. summarizing	A	O	S	N
d. questioning	A	O	S	N
e. genuineness	A	O	S	N
f. assertiveness	A	O	S	N
g. confrontation	A	O	S	N
h. problem solving	A	O	S	N

	Always	Often	Seldom	Never
44. I have continued (formally or informally) training for peer counseling	A	O	S	N
45. I feel I have adequate theoretical background to perform my peer counseling tasks	A	O	S	N
46. My activities are in keeping with a healthy life	A	O	S	N
47. I have developed my potentials as a person ...	A	O	S	N

PERSONAL DEVELOPMENT

	Always	Often	Seldom	Never
48. I abuse alcohol	A	O	S	N
49. I abuse chemicals	A	O	S	N

Personal Development (Continued)	Always	Often	Seldom	Never
50. I care about the welfare of others	A	O	S	N
51. I see myself as an equal to those I help	A	O	S	N
52. I feel positive about myself	A	O	S	N
53. I am aware of my strengths	A	O	S	N
54. I manage my stress effectively	A	O	S	N
55. I participate in a regular exercise program ...	A	O	S	N
56. I eat a balanced diet	A	O	S	N
57. I get an adequate amount of sleep	A	O	S	N
58. I know techniques for relaxation	A	O	S	N
59. I can perform the role of a leader	A	O	S	N
60. I practice my skills regularly	A	O	S	N
61. I get feedback for my skills from my supervisor	A	O	S	N
62. I read materials in the human relations area	A	O	S	N
63. I am interested in working with others in the peer counselor program as a team member ...	A	O	S	N
64. My interpersonal relationships with most other people are good	A	O	S	N
65. I am assertive in situations where people try to take advantage of me	A	O	S	N
66. I can confront people with their behavior if it is harmful to them	A	O	S	N
67. I get professional counseling if I am experiencing a serious problem	A	O	S	N

Personal Development (Continued)

	Always	Often	Seldom	Never
68. I feel comfortable in groups of people	A	O	S	N
69. I manage my time well	A	O	S	N
70. I become involved in more activities than I can manage	A	O	S	N
71. People can rely on me to be responsible	A	O	S	N
72. I operate ethically as a peer counselor	A	O	S	N
73. I have developed a Code of Conduct	A	O	S	N
74. I follow the Code of Ethics of my program	A	O	S	N

ADDITIONAL READINGS

Alberti, R.E., & Emmons, M.L. (1974). *Your perfect right: A guide to assertive behavior.* San Luis Obispo, CA Impact.

Anderson, R.A. (1978). *Stress power! How to turn tension into energy.* New York: Human Sciences Press.

Aronson, S., & Mascia, M. (1981). *The stress management workbook.* New York; Appleton Century Crofts.

Bartoletti, S., & Lisandrelli, E. (1988). *Study skills workout.* Glenview, IL: Scott, Foreman and Company.

Bauer, B., Anderson, W., & Hyatt, R. (1986). *Bulimia: A book for therapist and client.* Muncie, IN: Accelerated Development, Publishers.

Belloc, N.B., & Breslow, H. (1972). Relationship of physical health states and health practice. *Preventive Medicine, I,* 409-421.

Benson, H. (1975). *The relaxation response.* New York: Avon Publishers.

Black, C. (1982). *It will never happen to me!* Denver, CO: M.A.C. Publications.

Blanchard, K., & Lorder, R. (1984). *Putting the one minute manager to work.* New York: William Morrow.

Bowman, R.P. (Ed.) (1987). *Peer Facilitator Quarterly.* Minneapolis, MN: Educational Media Corporation.

Butler, J., & Bianchi, S. (1984). *Warm ups for meeting leaders.* Ventura, CA: Quality Group Publishing.

Capuzzi, D. (1986). Adolescent suicide: Prevention and intervention. *Counseling and Human Development, 19*(2).

Capuzzi, D. (1988, March & April). Causes of adolescent suicide, 2 parts. *Private Practice News, 2*(3,4) (575 Forest Avenue, Portland, ME 04101).

Capuzzi, D., & Golden, L. (1988). *Preventing adolescent suicide.* Muncie, IN: Accelerated Development, Publishers.

Carkhuff, R. (1973). *The art of helping.* Amherst, MA: Human Resources Development Press.

Carkhuff, R. (1973). *The art of problem solving.* Amherst, MA: Human Resources Development Press.

Cooper, J. (1977). *Aerobics.* New York: Bantam Books.

Corey, G., Corey, M., & Callahan, P. (1982). *A casebook of ethical guidelines for group leaders.* Monterey, CA: Brooks/Cole.

Davis, M., Eshelman, E. R., & McKay, M. (1980). *The relaxation and stress reduction workbook*. Richmond, CA: New Harbinger Publications.

Edelwich, J., & Brodsky, A. (1980). *Burn-out stages of disillusionment in the helping professions*. New York: Human Sciences Press.

Egan, G. (1975). *The skilled helper*. Monterey, CA: Brooks/Cole.

Ellis, A., & Harper, R.A. (1961). *A guide to rational living*. Englewood Cliffs, NJ: Prentice-Hall.

Foster, E.S. (1982). *Tutoring: Learning by helping*. Minneapolis, MN: Educational Media Corporation.

Frey, D., & Carlock, C.J. (1984). *Enhancing self esteem*. Muncie, IN: Accelerated Development, Publishers.

Gherman, E.M. (1981). *Stress and the bottom line*. New York: AMACOM.

Gordon, T. (1970). *Parent effectiveness training*. New York: Peter H. Wyden.

Gordon, T. (1977). *Leader effectiveness training*. New York: Bantam Books.

Greenberg, H. (1980). *Coping with job stress: A guide for all employers and employees*. Englewood Cliffs, NJ: Prentice-Hall.

Groger, M. (1983). *Eating awareness training. The natural way to permanent weight loss*. New York: Summit Books.

Hall, L., & Cohn, L. (1986). *A guide to recovery*. Carlsbad, CA: Gurze Books.

Hall, L., & Cohn, L. (1987). *Recoveries*. Carlsbad, CA: Gurze Books.

Hall, L., & Cohn, L. (1987). *True stories by people who conquered addictions and compulsions*. Carlsbad, CA: Gurze Books.

Harmon, M., Rugh, L., & Simon, S. (1966). *Values and teaching*. Columbus, OH: Merrill.

Harris, T. (1967). *I'm O.K., you're O.K*. New York: Avon Books.

Heinemann, M.E., & Estes, N.J. (1977). *Alcoholism development: Consequences and intervention*. St. Louis: The C.V. Mosby Company.

Hendricks, G., & Roberts, T. (1977). *The second centering book*. Englewood Cliffs, NJ: Prentice-Hall.

Hewett, J. (1980). *After suicide*. Philadelphia: Westminister Press.

Hollis, J. (1985). *Fat is a family affair*. Center City, MN: Hazelden.

Hollis, J. (1986). Suffering sabotage. *Shape, 6*(2).

Hoper, C., Kutzleb, U., Stobbe, A., & Weber, B. (1975). *Awareness games*. New York: St. Martin's Press.

Johnson, D. (1972). *Reaching out*. Englewood Cliffs, NJ: Prentice-Hall.

Jones, J., & Pfieffer, J.W. (1972). *A handbook of experiences for human relations training*. Iowa City, IA: University Associates.

Kano, S. (1985). *Making peace with food: A step-by-step guide to freedom from diet/weight conflict*. Danbury, CT: Amity Publishing

King, J. (1983). *Alcohol/drugs and kids: A handbook for parents*. St. Louis Area National Council on Alcoholism.

Kornblum, A. (1985, July). Suicide alert. *Harpers Bazaar.*

Krieg, F. (1988). *Group leadership training and supervision manual.* Muncie, IN: Accelerated Development, Publishers.

Kuepper, J. (1987). *Homework helpers: A guide for parents offering assistance.* Minneapolis, MN: Educational Media Corporation.

Lawson, L., Donant, F., & Lawson, J. (1982). *Lead on: The complete handbook for group leaders.* San Luis Obispo, CA: Impact Publishers.

Lengefel, U. (1987). *Study skills strategies.* Los Altos, CA: Cript Publications.

McKay, M., & Fanning, P. (1987). *Self esteem.* Oakland, CA: New Harbinger Publications.

Pease, V.P. (1981). *Anxiety into energy stress management.* New York: Hawthorn/Dutton.

Pelletier, K. (1977). *Holistic medicine from stress to optimum health.* New York: Dell Publishing.

Perez, J. (1984). *Counseling the alcoholic.* Muncie, IN: Accelerated Development, Publishers.

Phelps, S., & Austin, N. (1975). *The assertive woman.* San Luis Obispo, CA: Impact.

Raudsepp, E. (1985, July). Stress test for teens. *Harpers Bazaar.*

Rogers, C.H. (1980). *A way of being.* Boston: Houghton Mifflin.

Rosenfeld, L., & Prupas, M. (1984). *Left alive: After a suicide death in the family.* Springfield, IL: Charles C. Thomas.

Rosenthal, H. (1988). *Not with my life I don't: Preventing your suicide and that of others.* Muncie, IN: Accelerated Development, Publishers.

Sacker, I., & Zimmer, M. (1987). *Dying to be this: Understanding and defeating anorexia nervosa and bulimia.* New York: Warner Books.

Samuels, D., & Samuels, M. (1975). *The complete handbook of peer counseling.* Miami, FL: Fiesta Publishing.

Satir, V. (1972). *Peoplemaking.* Palo Alto, CA: Science and Behavior Books.

Sehnert, K.W. (1981). *Stress/unstress.* Minneapolis, MN: Augsburg Publishing House.

Selye, H. (1974). *Stress without distress.* New York: J.B. Lippincott.

Selye, H. (1978). *The stress of life (rev. ed.).* New York: McGraw-Hill.

Shipman, F. Student stress and sucide. *The Practitioner.* (NASSP newsletter for on-line administrators), 1904 Association Drive, Reston, VA 22091).

Simon, S. (1973). *I am lovable and capable (IALAC).* Allen, TX: Communications.

Standacher, C. (1988). *Beyond grief.* Oakland, CA: New Harbinger Publications.

Stein, P., & Unell, B. (1986). *Anorexia Nervosa.* Minneapolis, MN: CompCare Publications.

Thelan, H.A. (1954). *Dynamics of groups at work.* Chicago: University of Chicago Press.

Weyscheider, S. (1981). *Another Chance.* Palo Alto, CA: Science & Behavior Books, Inc.

Wolfelt, A. (1983). *Helping children cope with grief.* Muncie, IN: Accelerated Development, Publishers.

Woodman, M. (1982). *Addiction to perfection.* Toronto, Canada: Inner City Books.

FILMSTRIPS

Sunburst Communications, 39 Washington Avenue, Pleasantville, NY 10570:

Preventing teen suicide: "You Can Help" (filmstrip)

Coping with depression "Teenage Blues" (filmstrip and video)

ABOUT
THE
AUTHOR

JUDITH A. TINDALL

Psychologist

Counselor

Consultant

Author

Judith A. Tindall, Ph.D., has been involved in training peer counselors and supervisors in schools, and community agencies since 1969. For the last several years she has been in private practice as a psychologist and consultant with Rohen and Associates Psychological Center in St. Charles, Missouri. Prior to this she worked for 18 years in public schools as a counselor and guidance director. She has been a consultant to, and has conducted workshops with businesses, schools, church groups, and hospitals concerning a wide range of topics. She has consulted with such companies as Ralston Purina, Monsanto, McDonnell Douglas, TWA, and numerous schools, hospitals, and churches. She also has been on the staff of Webster University and the University of Missouri at St. Louis.

Dr. Tindall has been active in professional associations, holding offices and committee chairs at the local level (St. Louis Association of Counseling and Development, St. Louis Wellness Association, St. Louis Association of Training and Development), state level (Missouri Guidance Association and American Association for Counseling and Development and the National Peer Helper Association). She serves on the Board of the NPHA and is Ethics and Standards chairperson and was co-conference coordinator for the first Peer Helpers Conference in St. Charles. She is the co-author of two books, *Peer Counseling: In Depth Look at Training Peer Helpers* and *Peer Power: Book 1*, and author of *Book 2: Applying Peer Helper Skills* and an audio tape on *Problem Solving*.

Dr. Tindall received a B.S.Ed. degree in Speech and Political Science from Southwest Missouri State University, an M.S. from the University of Missouri at Columbia in Counseling, a Specialist degree in Counseling and Psychology from Southern Illinois University at Edwardsville, and a Ph.D. in Psychology from St. Louis University. She also has received extensive training in hypnosis, communication skills, drug and alcohol counseling, M.B.T.I. Adlerian counseling, career education, wellness, stress management, imagery, biofeedback, pain management, eating disorders, group skills, suicide intervention, and consulting. Research topics include **communication skills, stress management, self-esteem, problem-solving, wellness, eating disorders, and group work.**

Dr. Tindall resides in St. Louis with her husband and two sons. She maintains a private practice in counseling, consulting, and training. Dr. Tindall is proficient in training peer helpers and has authored numerous articles on the topic.